Economics LIVE!

Learning Economics the Collaborative Way

Diane Keenan
Cerritos College
Cerritos, California

and Mark H. Maier
Glendale College
Glendale, California

McGraw-Hill, Inc.
College Custom Series

New York St. Louis San Francisco Auckland Bogotá
Caracas Lisbon London Madrid Mexico Milan Montreal
New Delhi Paris San Juan Singapore Sydney Tokyo Toronto

ECONOMICS LIVE!
Learning Economics the Collaborative Way

3 4 5 6 7 8 9 0 BAW BAW 9 0 9 8 7 6 5

ISBN 0-07-075616-3

Editor: Julie Kehrwald

Graphics Design & Page Layout by
Jackson Park Lagoon,
Pasadena, California

Cover Design: Steven White

Printer/Binder: Bawden Printing Press

Economics LIVE!
Table of Contents

Activity #	Title	Page#	Topic Guide

Teams

First, make certain that all team members understand "The Dreaded Disease." Then answer the questions below. Have a spokesperson ready to explain your team's decision.

The Dreaded Disease

Imagine an island economy that is periodically struck by an epidemic disease that affects only children. From past experience the islanders found that the disease strikes randomly, affecting 80% of all children. They also discovered a preventive antidote that reduces the chance of death if it is taken before the disease strikes.

A child who has taken no doses of the antidote has a 90% chance of dying when he or she contracts the disease. With one dose of the antidote, the chance of death is reduced to 10%. Two doses reduce the chance to 8%; three doses reduce the chance to 6%; four doses reduce the chance to 5%. Beyond four doses, the antidote has no further effect, and the chance of death remains at 5%.

Suppose the island has 1000 children and that at the first sign of a new outbreak of the dreaded disease, the people have produced 1000 doses. The antidote must be used immediately if the children's lives are to be saved.

The Dreaded Disease

Questions:

1. What would be a "market" solution to the problem?

   a. What would be the benefits of this solution?
   - for families with children?
   - for families without children?
   - for pharmaceutical companies?
   - for the economy?

   b. What would be the opportunity cost of this solution?

2. What would be a "command" solution to this problem?

   a. What would be the benefits of a command solution?

   b. What would be the opportunity costs?

continued

3. Which solution would your team choose? Why?

Medical care in the U.S.

Teams

Pass this sheet of paper around your team. Each team member writes down one idea, then passes it on.

Examples of market allocation of medical care in the U.S. today:

1.

2.

3.

Examples of non-market allocation of medical care in the U.S. today:

1.

2.

3.

Poll your teammates on the following question: Do you think medical care should be treated as a product--such as clothing or food--or a 'right' for everyone?

Teams

Your team will survey your classmates' willingness to buy one of the following goods or services (to be assigned by your instructor):

- one hour tutoring for this class
- 1990 Honda Accord with 75,000 miles
- copies of previous exams for the class
- pre-packed lunch (sandwich, fruit, drink)
- calculator wrist watch

- tuition for one semester
- guaranteed parking space
- note taking service
- 13" color TV
- 1 hour typing

Surveying Demand

Step 1

Given your team's product, brainstorm the possible ranges of prices for it.

What is the highest price someone would pay for it? _____

Agree on a range of five prices, from your low price to high price?

_____, _____, _____, _____, _____

Step 2

Now survey 10 other students. Ask them how many they would be willing to buy at each price.

Step 3

Now calculate the market demand (the sum of all individual demands.)

Price $ _____   Quantity demanded _____
Price $ _____   Quantity demanded _____
Price $ _____   Quantity demanded _____
Price $ _____   Quantity demanded _____
Price $ _____   Quantity demanded _____

Step 4

Construct a market demand curve based on your data.

PRICE

QUANTITY

Step 5

Identify when you used the concept of *ceteris paribus* during your survey.

Economics
LIVE / 3

© Keenan & Maier

Supply

Activity #3

Will you supply your labor?

Teams

You will survey other students in your group about their willingness to provide tutoring services on your college campus.

Step 1

Before you consult your teammates, think to yourself how many hours per week you would be willing to work at the following rates of pay.

$25/hr _____ hours
$20/hr _____ hours
$15/hr _____ hours
$10/hr _____ hours
$ 5/hr _____ hours

Step 2

Report your hours to your group. Have the team add up the total hours of all group members.

$25/hr _____ hours total for all team members
$20/hr _____ hours total for all team members
$15/hr _____ hours total for all team members
$10/hr _____ hours total for all team members
$ 5/hr _____ hours total for all team members

PRICE (wage)

$25

$20

$15

$10

$ 5

QUANTITY
(# of hours)

Step 3

Construct a market supply curve for your group for tutoring services.

Step 4

How does your supply curve compare with those in your textbook? Does it conform to the Law of Supply?

Step 5

Which member of your group was willing to tutor the least hours at the highest pay rate? Interview this person about his/her choices. See if you can identify the idea of **opportunity cost** in his/her answer.

Attention, Buyers and Sellers of Black Pearls!

Black pearls from the island of Bliss are valued all over the world. Buyers and sellers of these exotic pearls meet at the Pearl Exchange, located right here in this classroom. You will buy or sell black pearls during the trading sessions. Your goal is to make as much money as you can. Before each trading session begins, you draw a buyer or seller card.

Buyers:

Try to buy the pearls as inexpensively as you can. Buying for less than the amount on the card saves money.

Sellers:

Try to sell the pearls for as much as you can. Selling for more than the amount on the card creates a profit.

There will be four trading sessions. When you make a deal, shake hands, come to the board and tell the recorder the selling price. Go back to your seat and record your profit or loss. If you don't make a sale or purchase, take the entire amount on your card as a loss.

Good luck!

Buying and Selling Black Pearls

Round	Card Price	Price Purchased or Sold	Profit (Loss)
1	$_____	$_____	$_____
2	$_____	$_____	$_____
3	$_____	$_____	$_____
4	$_____	$_____	$_____

continued

Demand and supply schedule

Complete the schedule below and determine the equilibrium price.

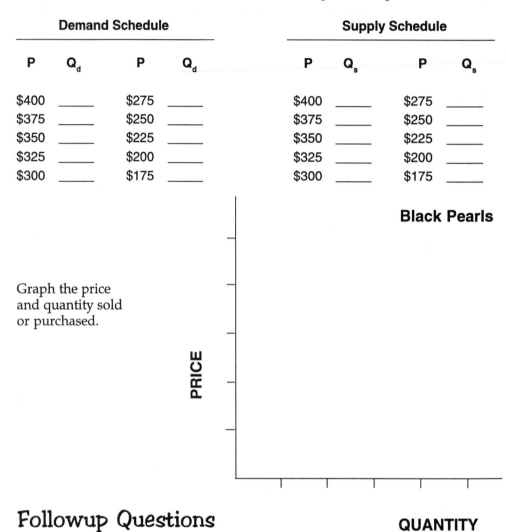

Demand Schedule

P	Q$_d$	P	Q$_d$
$400	_____	$275	_____
$375	_____	$250	_____
$350	_____	$225	_____
$325	_____	$200	_____
$300	_____	$175	_____

Supply Schedule

P	Q$_s$	P	Q$_s$
$400	_____	$275	_____
$375	_____	$250	_____
$350	_____	$225	_____
$325	_____	$200	_____
$300	_____	$175	_____

Black Pearls

Graph the price
and quantity sold
or purchased.

PRICE

QUANTITY

Followup Questions

1. What is the equilibrium price?

2. If the game were played for a long time, why would **all** pearls sell at this equilibrium price?

3. If sellers insisted on a price of $400, how much of a surplus would be created?

4. If sellers priced at $175, how much of a shortage would be created?

Teams

After reading the article on the following page, each team member will write down one factor in the article that deals with supply or demand. Pass this sheet on to the next person. Pass it around your team at least three times.

Demand	Supply
_____	_____
_____	_____
_____	_____
_____	_____
_____	_____
_____	_____
_____	_____
_____	_____
_____	_____

Demand for Fast Food in South Korea

Questions

Put your heads together and answer the following:

1. According to the article, the United States fast food market is "oversaturated." What does that mean? Show it graphically with a supply and demand graph.

2. If all fast food firms in South Korea face high land costs, what would that do to supply? Show graphically.

3. How have sellers in the South Korean fast food market managed to avoid high land costs?

4. Overall, what is happening to the supply of fast food in South Korea? Demand? Show both together in one supply and demand graph.

5. Given your analysis above, what do you predict for:
   a. the price of fast food in South Korea?

   b. profits of fast food firms in South Korea?

   c. quantity of fast food sold in South Korea?

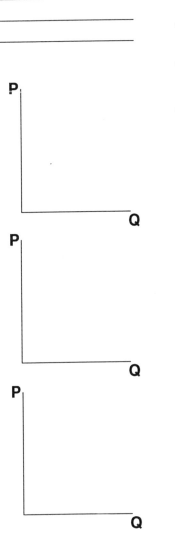

continued

South Koreans Crave American Fast Food

Fast-Food Firms Find Potential for Fast Growth in South Korea

by Damon Darlin, *The Wall Street Journal*, February 22, 1992

SEOUL, South Korea - Moon Yong, a 21-year-old college student, loves fast food. So much so that, like hundreds of Korean girls, she comes to a fast food restaurant every afternoon. Today she is at Hardee's nibbling on French fries and sipping Cokes with a friend.

For Korean kids, fast-food restaurants are the trendy places to hang out. "We'll stay here all afternoon," she says. Tomorrow it may be Kentucky Fried Chicken or McDonald's. Her only complaint: "There should be more fast-food restaurants."

American fast-food companies are discovering the same thing. South Korea, the largest consumer market in Asia outside of Japan, has fewer fast-food stands per capita than other Asian countries of a comparable economic level. Competition is tough in the oversaturated U.S. market and getting tougher in the developing markets of Japan and Hong Kong, but Korea is virtually unexplored territory for fast-food marketers.

Slow Entry

The Korean fast-food market is tiny but booming. Revenues doubled last year to about $615 million, and are expected to grow anywhere from 50% to 100% annually for the next several years. Moreover, per store sales average twice the U.S. level.

Despite that promise, McDonald's Corp. has moved into Korea much more slowly than into many other overseas markets. The nation has only four McDonald's for a population of 43 million, compared with 51 restaurants for 5.7 million residents of Hong Kong, the region's most McDonald's-saturated economy.

So, Korea is a land of opportunity for other fast-food companies, even those that have barely any presence in other overseas markets and flat sales in the U.S. Wendy's International Inc. has 13 outlets in Korea, and Burger King Corp. has 12; both plan to add about five or six restaurants a year for the next several years. Hardee's Food Systems Inc., the No. 3 hamburger chain in the U.S. has just two stores in Korea now, but plans to add six to eight a year. Del Taco Korea Col, a Mexican-food chain is also planning rapid expansion here with the help of a Korean-American entrepreneur.

For most American fast-food companies, overseas expansion is the fastest way to grow. "We look at some [Asian] countries as being in the same situation the U.S. was in during the 1960s," says George Rice, a fast-food consultant in Chicago. "We are looking at tremendous growth [in Asia.]

But Korea is a tough market. Land prices are high. A heavy-traffic site in Seoul can cost about $7 million to buy or requires a deposit of $1 million to rent. Raw-material costs are the highest in Asia, says a McDonald's internal survey. Government restrictions, such as high tariffs and limits on cheese and beef imports are frustrating.

Hardee's thinks it has figured out a way to trump McDonald's in Korea and avoid some of the business problems. It sold its Korea franchise to Kim Chang-Hwan, a wealthy local businessman. Mr. Kim's older brother runs a retail shoe chain that has many stores near student hangouts--fertile ground for fast-food. So the Kims are converting several of the shoe stores into restaurants. "We have a chance of being a very major player because McDonald's is weak," says manager of the Korean franchisee, Seijin Food Systems Inc.

Near Rivals

The Korean Hardee's showed its chutzpah by opening its first restaurant just a few yards from a popular McDonald's in downtown Seoul. Mr. Kang says Hardee's executives had strong reservations about the strategy. But so far, he says, the store's sales are equal to the neighboring McDonald's.

Kim Dae-Hwan, marketing manager for McDonald's Korea says, "We are always full, so [people] go down the street." Nevertheless, McDonald's is feeling the pressure and planning to step up its expansion. In 1986, the company formed a 50-50 joint venture with a Korean accountant. It had planned to have 14 stores open by now.

But it didn't open its first store until 1988, and expansion has been slow. Some say it is because Mr. Ahn, who died earlier this month, had been seriously ill for about a year. A McDonald's spokesman in the U.S. says the company is uncertain what it will do about a local partner.

Local employees also say McDonald's Korea, initially undercapitalized, balked at the price of Korean real estate. Its policy was to buy a site or lease it long term. But with real-estate prices and rents rising more than 50% a year, speculators don't sell or even lease long term.

Now McDonald's seems to understand the costs of real estate here. "McDonald's people say we have to be more aggressive on expansion," says Jun Eung Jun, operations manager at McDonald's Korea. Officials now say the company will have 300 restaurants in Korea by the end of 1993.

The McDonald's spokesman in the U.S. doesn't disagree with the local staff's opinions, but he says, "We move very cautiously. It is deliberate because of the infrastructure we need to develop. It is just [a matter of] being very certain that everything is in place."

The target market in Korea for fast food is young people and about 70% of customers are young girls. That skews the sales. About 15% of sales are French fries, 35% are beverages. (And because the girls stay there for hours, the restaurants are usually big: 300 seats, or about twice the U.S. size.)

Despite strong anti-American sentiment in Korea these days, it's the slice of American life that attracts kids to fast-food restaurants. "They like American and European music," says Young Lee, president of Del Taco Korea Co. "So they want their food the say way. It is this area that America is the leader, not electric parts or TV." Del Taco Korea, a franchise of American Restaurant Group Inc. in Newport Beach, Calif., presents its food as American or Californian, not Mexican, and Koreans are responding strongly to what, for them, is unusual food.

Fast-food chains make subtle changes to account for local tastes, but there is less adaption than in some of the Asian countries. Menus tend to be all-American. Del Taco's Mr. Lee tried to come as close to the real Monterey Jack cheese taste with local products, because the government won't let him import the real thing. He altered his chain's taco sauce to make it more like Korean pepper sauce, but that's as far as he has tinkered. Referring to a Korean dish of fiery fermented cabbage, Mr. Lee says, "We can't change 100% to a kimchi taco."

Teams

Pick a partner. Person "A" does odd numbers while person "B" coaches. Then "B" does the even numbers while "A" coaches.

Graph the following statements

Be sure to distinguish between a price effect *(a movement along the demand curve)* and other factors that influence demand like tastes and income. *(These shift the demand curve.)*

Curbing smoking

1. In 1971, cigarette advertising was banned from television in the United States. Fewer teenagers smoke.

2. Cigarette taxes in the United States have caused the average price to rise from $.76 to $1.10 a pack. As a result, 2 million Americans quit smoking.

3. In Poland, cigarettes are priced at just 22 zlotys ($.67), far less than in the U.S. Poland has one of the highest consumption levels for cigarettes.

4. Smoking in the United States is prohibited in many public places. Smokers are finding it more difficult to smoke.

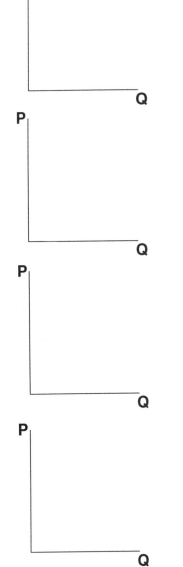

Moving along and shifting those demand curves

continued

Skiing

5. Last December, Mammoth Mountain Ski Resort in California had very little snow and few skiers.

6. In 1991, Mammoth Mountain raised its ticket price from $40 to $46 a day. As a result, ticket sales fell.

Videos and movies

7. As the price of movies goes up the sales of video rentals soar. (Show both movie and video rental markets.)

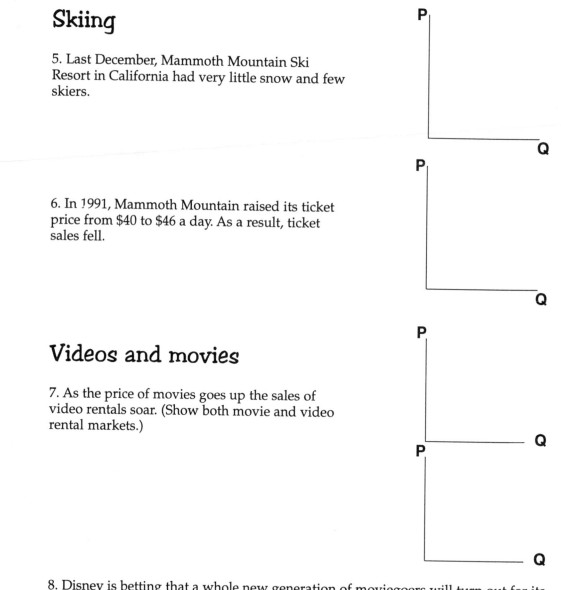

8. Disney is betting that a whole new generation of moviegoers will turn out for its re-release of the film Pinocchio, despite the fact that the film has already been released for sale on video cassette. Does the company see them as substitutes or complements?

Based on your answer to the question above, show both markets graphically.

Teams

Pick a partner. Person "A" does odd numbers while "B" coaches. Then "B" does the even numbers while "A" coaches.

Graph the following statements

Be sure to distinguish between a price effect **(a movement along the supply curve)** and other factors that influence supply such as weather or the costs of production. **(These are shifts in supply.)**

Oil

1. At the beginning of the Persian Gulf War, both Iraqi and Kuwaiti oil was removed from the market. The price of crude oil jumped from $19 to $40 per barrel.

2. Later, Saudi Arabia and Venezuela increased their oil production. The price of crude oil fell to $22 per barrel.

3. As a result of lower prices, oil exploration in the United States decreased.

Moving along and shifting those supply curves

continued

4. Many of the wells in the United States have been tapped out with vertical drilling. Producers have had to use more expensive horizontal drilling equipment. As a result, the costs of production are higher in the United States than in Saudi Arabia. **(Show the U.S. and Saudi oil markets.)**

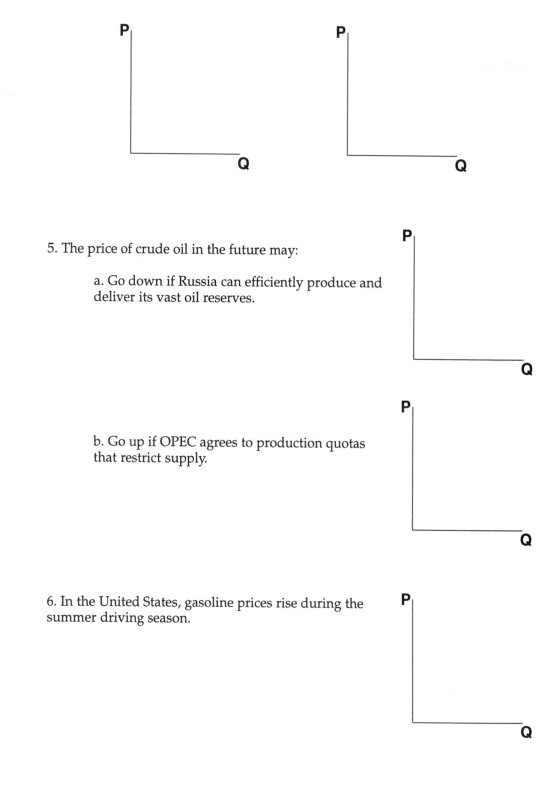

5. The price of crude oil in the future may:

a. Go down if Russia can efficiently produce and deliver its vast oil reserves.

b. Go up if OPEC agrees to production quotas that restrict supply.

6. In the United States, gasoline prices rise during the summer driving season.

Teams

Pair off. Person A writes explanation on odd problems while B graphs it. Person B writes explanation on even problems while A graphs it.

Explain in words and use a graph for the following:

Putting it all together

1. Why water, which is essential for life, is cheaper than diamonds.

P

Q

P

Q

2. Why the price of lumber shot up following Hurricane Andrew in Florida.

P

Q

3. Why hockey hero Wayne Gretsky is paid more than a fast food worker.

P

Q

P

Q

4. Why superbowl tickets can go as high as $500.

P

Q

continued

5. At the end of the season, the hapless Seattle Mariners baseball team has many empty seats.

P

Q

6. The price of VCRs has dropped from $800 when they were first introduced to their average price of $200 today.

P

Q

7. To attract new customers a supermarket sells soda pop at less than cost, but then must supply rainchecks--the promise to sell the low-price soda pop at a later time because supplies run out.

P

Q

8. Why a mint condition Mickey Mantle baseball card can go as high as $27,000.

P

Q

9. Why, as more lenders offer credit cards, interest rates on the cards fall.

P

Q

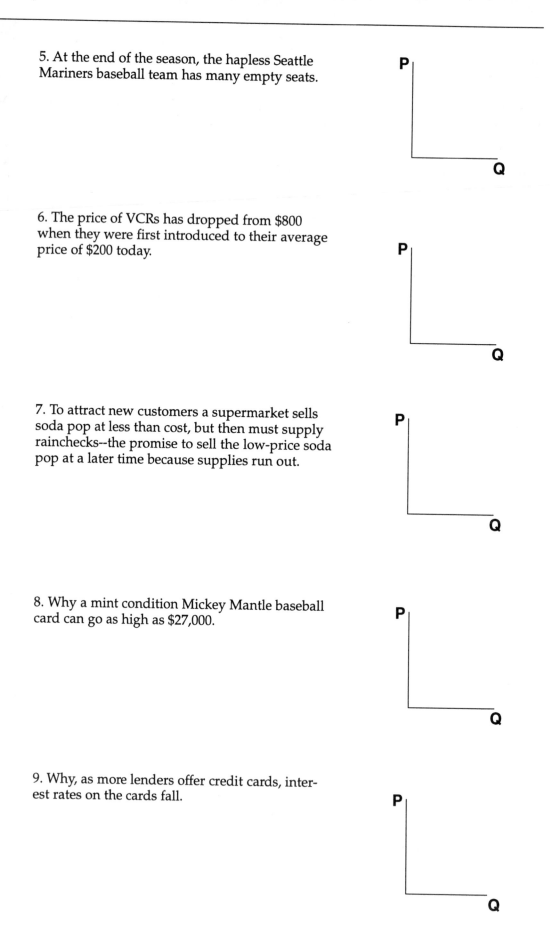

Teams

Choose a spokesperson for your team. Brainstorm the answers to the following questions together. Make sure your spokesperson is ready to defend your answers.

1. Economists estimate that the price elasticity of demand for heroin is 0.4. What does that mean? Show the demand for heroin graphically.

P

Q

Elasticity and the demand for drugs

2. Efforts to limit the supply of heroin has had little impact on the quantity demanded for heroin. Why? Show graphically.

P

Q

3. Doubling federal law enforcement efforts to block heroin imports is estimated to raise its price by 13%. By what percentage would quantity sold fall?   (Use the formula for elasticity in your textbook.)

4. If the price of heroin rises, given its inelastic demand, what happens to the incomes of heroin dealers?

5. The price elasticity of demand for marijuana is estimated to be 1.5. What does that mean? Why is demand for marijuana more price elastic than heroin?

continued

Economics
LIVE / 15

© Keenan & Maier

6. If the price of marijuana rises by 10%, by what percentage would quantity sold fall?

7. Efforts to raise the price of drugs to discourage use would be most effective against heroin or marijuana?

8. Brainstorm a list of all possible methods to reduce drug use in the U.S.

Methods to Reduce Demand	Methods to Restrict Supply
_____	_____
_____	_____
_____	_____
_____	_____
_____	_____
_____	_____
_____	_____
_____	_____
_____	_____
_____	_____
_____	_____
_____	_____

In your team's opinion, which approach would be most effective? Why?

Teams

Your group will be assigned one good or service. Your goal is to estimate the price elasticity of demand for it.

Step 1

Write out the formula for elasticity of demand:

Estimating Elasticity of Demand

Step 2

In your own group, find out what is the highest price at which **only** one person will buy this product?

(Write down P1 = _____   Qd1 = ___1___)

Lower the price so that **at least** one more person in your group will buy this product.

(Write down P2 = _____   Qd2 = _____)

Step 3

Given these two prices, survey students in one other group as to their willingness to buy. Total the quantity demanded at these prices, including your group as well as the other students you surveyed.

P1 = _____   Qd1 = _____   P2 = _____   Qd2 = _____

Step 4

1. Now calculate the price elasticity of demand.

2. Is demand in this case elastic or inelastic?

3. What factors might explain why it is elastic or inelastic?

4. How does it compare with other elasticities listed in your textbook?

M&Ms and Marginal Utility

Teams

Bring one bag of M&Ms to class. Ask one member of your group to be the test subject. Ask this person to rank the additional satisfaction for M&Ms on a 1-10 scale (10 begin the highest level of satisfaction.) Given this person one M&M at a time and record his or her marginal utility.

# of M&Ms	Marginal Utility	# of M&Ms	Marginal Utility
1	_____	6	_____
2	_____	7	_____
3	_____	8	_____
4	_____	9	_____
5	_____	10	_____

As a group answer the following:

1. What happened to marginal utility as more M&Ms were consumed?

2. When did diminishing marginal utility begin?

3. Does the test confirm the law of diminishing marginal utility?

4. What happened to total utility during the test?

5. Write one paragraph that explains the relationship between the concept of diminishing marginal utility and consumers' willingness to pay high or low prices.

6. Use the theory of marginal utility to explain the following:
   a. Why people buy a variety of products.

   b. Why people buy *one* refrigerator or *one* house.

   c. Why water, which is essential for life, is cheaper than diamonds.

   d. Why we spend more time hunting for the best price for larger purchases than for smaller ones.

Teams

You must reach a majority consensus in your team on the following statements based on the article, "Urban Consumers Pay More," from the *Wall Street Journal*, July 2, 1992. Are they true or false? Be ready to defend your team's position.

1. W. Jean Shelby is a rational consumer.

2. Ms. Shelby is maximizing her total satisfaction given her limited budget.

3. Ms. Shelby prefers current consumption to future consumption.

4. Ms. Shelby's behavior can be explained by the fact that she does not have complete information.

5. Prices are higher in the inner city because demand is more inelastic.

6. Prices are higher in the inner city because the costs of doing business are higher there.

7. Supply usually follows demand, but not in the inner cities of the United States. This indicates that capitalism is not working well.

8. **(Optional)** Using the indifference curve approach, Ms. Shelby's preferences would look like which graph, U_1 or U_2?

Are consumers rational?

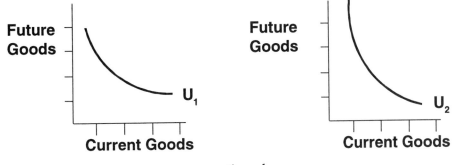

continued

© Keenan & Maier

Poverty's Cost:

Urban Consumers Pay More and Get Less And Gap May Widen

By Francine Schwadel, *The Wall Street Journal,* July 2, 1992

CHICAGO -- For many Americans, catalog shopping means Victoria's Secret, Sharper Images or Land's End. But poor people like W. Jean Shelby get Fingerhut Catalogs, where the bold face price isn't the total price but the amount per month.

One recent offer:"TV/VCR combination, $56.64 per month." The deal appealed to Mrs. Shelby, who supports herself and four children on $597 a month from her part time job, food stamps and $422 in Supplemental Social Security for one child. She bought the set, committing herself to 19 monthly payments that won't end [for more than a year]. The total she will pay, including finance charges at 24.9% annual rate: $1,133.16. The same set can be found in the suburbs for as little as $499.

Why not save up and buy the set outright? "I want things right away," Mrs. Shelby says. She also points out that she could lose her food stamps and Medicaid benefits if she saves too much. State officials say she could save up to $2,000, but Mrs. Shelby thinks the cap is $500. In any case, the restrictions on savings help create a *carpe diem* consumerism in the inner city, where the basic law of supply and demand sometimes seems to break down: There is tremendous demand for goods by people like Mrs. Shelby, but often not enough interested merchants.

Except for in some urban areas in which large chains have made special efforts, being a consumer in the inner city isn't like being a consumer in the suburbs. Prices are higher, selections are more limited. Because Mrs. Shelby doesn't have a car, she pays extra to have her groceries delivered. When she is short of cash and asks to pay the delivery charge with food stamps, the fee goes up $1. Because few stores in her area sell clothes and none specializes in toys, buying these items means paying to travel by bus to a more lively shopping district.

The discount stores, outlet malls and warehouse clubs that have redefined suburbia's idea of a bargain have largely by-passed inner-city neighborhoods like Mrs. Shelby's. These retailers see bigger opportunities in serving the more-affluent middle class. The inner city is "a much harder market to make money in" because of higher costs for insurance and security and larger loss to theft, says Carl Steidtmann, chief economist at the Management Horizons retail consulting unit of Price Waterhouse. For this and other reasons he gave, differences between prices paid by the rich and poor appear to be widening at the same time the income gap is growing. Last year, the New York City Department of Consumer Affairs found that grocery shoppers in poor neighborhoods paid 8.8% more-or $350 more a year for a family of four-than did shoppers in middle-class areas. In Chicago, City Council staffers did a spot check of five items last year and found that the poor paid 18% more.

The problem, of course, isn't entirely one of exploitation. People in the inner city tend not to be skilled consumers. Ms. Shelby, for instance, pays more than $40 a month for local phone service-twice the national average-because she gets so many optional services, including the most expensive maintenance package Illinois Bell offers. She also pays more than $50 a month for cable television service, though she acknowledges that she doesn't really need two cable hookups and three movie channels.

But most of the problems aren't of Ms. Shelby's making. Finance charges for the poor, for instance, have soared in recent years because of the deregulating of consumer interest rates in many states. Today, it isn't uncommon for the poor to pay annual rates of 40% or 45%, says Alan Alop, director of consumer litigation for the Legal Assistance Foundation of Chicago. In two state-court suits filed on behalf of low-income clients, foundation lawyers are arguing that such rates are "unconscionable." The defendants: two car dealers and a finance company that charge 50%.

Low-income consumers could avoid such fees by saving to make big-ticket purchases in cash. But even those who don't fear losing government benefits have trouble saving. The poorest 10% of American's typically devote 70% of their budgets to food, housing, utilities and medical expenses.

Ms. Shelby, 42, dropped out of high school in the 10th grade when she became pregnant with her first of her five children. She spent several years on welfare, feeling depressed and "caged in." Things started improving four years ago when she joined a local church and landed a part time job as a janitor for a neighborhood social-service organization called Circle Urban Ministries. Eventually she worked her way up to receptionist.

Hertz Corporation Study

Los Angeles Times, January 23, 1984

For only the second time in history, the per-mile cost of owning and operating a typical new compact car dropped in 1983 by 1.4 cents to 43.28 cents, an annual Hertz Corp. study showed Sunday.

The 43.28 cents per mile driving cost was calculated based on a compact domestic sedan, such as the Ford Fairmont, driven 10,000 miles a year for five years.

The figure included fixed costs comprised of depreciation, 13.71 cents; insurance and license fees, 9.98 cents and interest, 7.66 cents. Variable costs included maintenance and repairs, 3.55 cents and gasoline, 8.38 cents.

The Cost of Owning a Car

Teams

As a team calculate the following:

1. If you drive the car for 10,000 miles, what are the AFC per mile? _____.
Now calculate the total fixed costs (AFC x 10,000) = _____. If you drive only 5,000 miles, your total fixed costs will be the same. Therefore the AFC per mile for driving 5,000 miles is (total fixed costs/5000) = _____.

2. Compute and fill in the missing values:

Q of Miles	AFC	AVC	ATC	TC	MC
5,000	_____	11.93¢	_____	_____	
					> _____
10,000	_____	11.93¢	_____	_____	
					> _____
15,000	_____	11.93¢	_____	_____	

Assume that the average variable costs of running the car (gas, oil etc.) stay constant from 5,000 to 15,000 miles.

3. Show ATC and AFC graphically.

4. Let's say you drive this car 10,000 miles. If your boss offers you a job driving at a reimbursement of 20 cents per mile, would you do it? Why or why not?

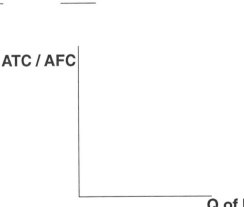

5. Would ATC eventually rise? Why or why not?

6. At what point do you think Hertz will sell this Ford Fairmont? Why?

Costs

Activity #14

Producing the "Midi"

Teams

Pick a partner. Person "A" does the odd numbers, while person "B" coaches. Then "B" does the even numbers while "A" coaches.

You are in charge of an automobile plant making a sports car called the "Midi." Your engineering department estimates your costs of production at:

You are told that you can sell up to 10,000 cars a month at a price of $10,000 each.

Quantity (# of cars)	Marginal Costs
5,000	$8,000
5,500	8,500
6,000	9,000
6,500	10,000
7,000	12,000

1. What is your marginal revenue per car? $_____

2. By increasing your production from 5,000 cars per month to 5,001 cars, would you increase your profits? _____   to 6,000 cars ? _____   to 6,500 cars? _____ to 7,000 cars? _____

3. The rule for profit maximization is to produce the quantity of cars where _____equals _____.

4. Why do marginal costs increase?

5. What would you do if the demand for these cars increased so that could sell them for $10,500? (Show graphically for the Midi market and for car market as a whole.)

Midi

P

Q

Car Market

P

Q

6. What if your workers gain an increase in their wages? What would happen to your average costs?   What would happen to your level of production?

7. Given your higher wage bill, why might you not be able to increase price?

On the other hand, why might the price in the entire car market rise? Show graphically, assuming all firms face increased wages.

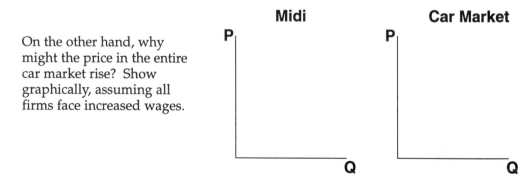

Midi

P

Q

Car Market

P

Q

Teams

Organize into groups of three. Number off "1," "2" and "3." Imagine that you are just starting college and you must decide what kind of typewriter to buy (your choice: manual or electronic typewriter or a computer).

Person 1

You have purchased a manual typewriter for $100. It costs you $3 per page to hire a typist to use this machine.

Calculate your costs:

# of Pages	FC (machine)	VC (labor)	TC ($)	ATC ($ per page)
30	___	___	___	___
50	___	___	___	___
100	___	___	___	___
500	___	___	___	___
1000	___	___	___	___
2000	___	___	___	___

Graph the ATC:

Typing and Economies of Scale

Person 2

You have purchased the electronic typewriter for $200. It costs you $1.50 per page to hire a typist to use this machine.

# of Pages	FC (machine)	VC (labor)	TC ($)	ATC ($ per page)
30	___	___	___	___
50	___	___	___	___
100	___	___	___	___
500	___	___	___	___
1000	___	___	___	___
2000	___	___	___	___

Graph the ATC:

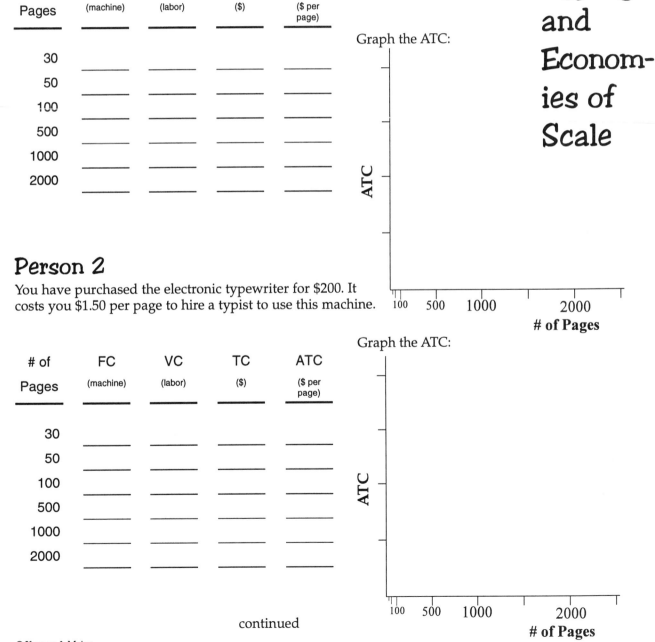

continued

Person 3

You have purchased a computer for $1000. It costs you $.50 per page to hire a typist to use this machine.

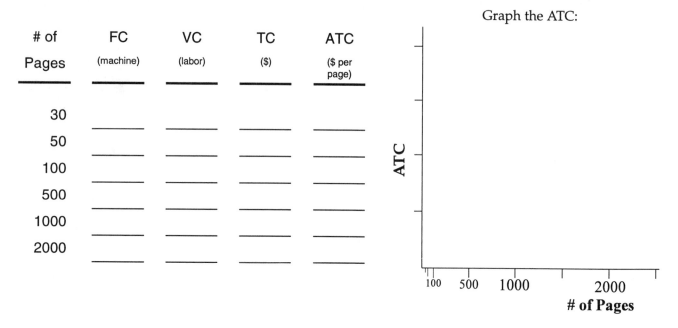

Graph the ATC:

# of Pages	FC (machine)	VC (labor)	TC ($)	ATC ($ per page)
30				
50				
100				
500				
1000				
2000				

When you complete your table and graph, rejoin the group. As a group answer the following:

1. Complete this table:

Pages	Which Machine is Least Expensive	Average Total Cost (ATC)
30		
50		
100		
500		
1000		
2000		

2. Now add the two other ATC curves to your own. In a different color, identify the *long-run* ATC curve, assuming that inputs (machines) can be changed.

3. How is the LRATC curve different from your individual ATC curve?

4. In this case, were there economies of scale or diseconomies of scale? Explain.

Teams

Divide your team into 3 groups. Group 1 does Exercise #1, group 2 does #2 and group 3 does #3.

Exercise 1

The Organize It! notebook company has the following revenues and costs:

1. What do the abbreviations Q, TR and TC stand for?

2. Define TR and TC:

3. How much are the company's fixed costs?

Q	TR	TC	Total Profit
0	$0	$10	_____
1	15	20	_____
2	30	28	_____
3	45	38	_____
4	60	50	_____
5	75	65	_____
6	90	85	_____

Calculate total profits at each level of output. At what level of output are profits maximized? _____

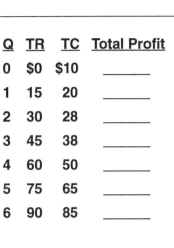

Profits at Organize It!

Exercise 2

The Organize It! notebook company has the following information:

1. What do the abbreviations Q, MR and MC stand for?

2. Define MR and MC:

Q		MR	MC
0			
	>	$15	$10
1			
	>	15	8
2			
	>	15	10
3			
	>	15	12
4			
	>	15	15
5			
	>	15	20
6			

3. Based on the profit-maximizing rule, at what level of output are profits maximized?

continued

© Keenan & Maier

Exercise 3

The **Organize It!** notebook company has the following revenues and costs.

Q	TR	MR	TC	MC
0	$0		$10	
		> _____		> _____
1	15		20	
		> _____		> _____
2	30		28	
		> _____		> _____
3	45		38	
		> _____		> _____
4	60		50	
		> _____		> _____
5	75		65	
		> _____		> _____
6	90		85	

1. What do the abbreviations TR, MR, TC and MC stand for?

2. Define MR and MC:

3. Calculate MR and MC from the information given and fill in the blanks.

Teams

Come together after your 3 groups have completed their exercises.

1. Share your results. Does everyone agree with your calculation of MR, MC, TC, TR and profit maximization?

2. What are the two ways for finding the profit-maximizing level of output?

The Sagetax Company is a small corporation that has an office with a computer and other office equipment. A secretary handles correspondence, answers the phone, schedules appointments and does general office work. The company's fixed costs are items such as office space, office equipment and the secretary's services. The fixed costs are $288 per week. The variable cost is the number of hours worked by the owners. Each owner's time is valued at $8 per hour.

The Sagetax Company

Tax returns per week (Q)	Owners Time	TFC	TVC	TC	MC	AFC	AVC	ATC	___	___
0	0	—	—	—		—	—	—		
					>__					
10	6	—	—	—		—	—	—		
					>__					
20	10	—	—	—		—	—	—		
					>__					
30	13	—	—	—		—	—	—		
					>__					
40	17	—	—	—		—	—	—		
					>__					
50	24	—	—	—		—	—	—		
					>__					
60	36	—	—	—		—	—	—		
					>__					
70	55	—	—	—		—	—	—		
					>__					
80	83	—	—	—		—	—	—		

Teams

Step 1

Individually solve the problem above, filling in the blank spaces. Remember that MC = ΔTC / ΔQ

Step 2

Meet as a team to share your results. Correct any errors.

Step 3

In the space on the following page, graph MC, AFC and ATC.

Explain why AFC falls and MC turns upwards.

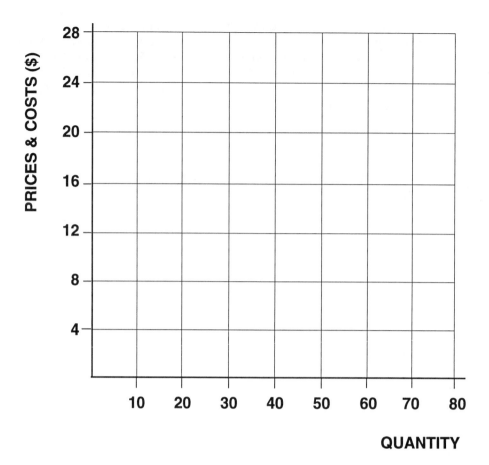

PRICES & COSTS ($)

28
24
20
16
12
8
4

10 20 30 40 50 60 70 80

QUANTITY

Step 4
Assume that Sagetax is a price taker and can sell all it wants at a price of $10. Add a column for total revenue to the table, and fill in the total revenue for each Q.

Step 5
Add P=MR line to your graph above, and find the profit-maximizing level of output.

Step 6
Add a column for **Profit** for each Q on the table (TR - TC = Total Profit). What are the profits for the level of output you chose in Step 5. Is it the same as your answer to step 4?

> (If the Q is in between two numbers, you can find TC from the formula TC = Q x ATC that output.)

Step 7
Is Sagetax earning a normal profit, an economic profit or an economic loss? How can you tell?

Step 8
Will there be entry or exit of firms in this industry?

Teams

Each member of your group should have read the article "A Nose for Profit." As a team identify:

Name of company: _____ Type of business ownership:
_____ Type of market structure (perfect competition, oligopoly etc.): _____

Now divide your group into 2 smaller groups (A and B).

Group A -- Step 1

Write down everything in the article having to do with: **Cost of production (inputs, efficiencies, inefficiencies, marginal costs, technology, economies of scale, cost minimizing strategies)**

Group B -- Step 1

Write down everything in the article having to do with: **Revenues and profits (revenues, competitors, market share, demand, profit maximizing strategies, profit or loss)**

Group A -- Step 2

Determine the major issue having to do with costs of production. When you agree, describe it to group B.

Group B -- Step 2

Determine the major issue having to do with revenues. When you agree, describe it to group A.

Groups A & B -- Step 3

Try to graph these issues facing the company.

Before you can do this, you must decide:
• Is this firm a price taker or price searcher? What will the marginal revenue curve look like?

continued

A
Nose
for
Profit

- What will the ATC curve look like? Is the firm enjoying economies of scale?

Firm

Market

Groups A & B -- Step 4

Be ready to explain your model and how it illustrates the major issues facing your firm.

A Nose for Profit: 'Pinocchio' Release to Test Truth of Video Sales Theory

By Kathryn Harris, *Los Angeles Times*, June 12, 1992

In a summertime ritual, Walt Disney Co. is readying another animated classic for re-release in theatres, 7 and 1/2 years after the movie's last appearance on a marquee. "Pinocchio," the 1940 film has ben spiffed up by a restoration team for its seventh outing on June 26th.

But Disney executives will be looking closely at the film for other reasons. "Pinocchio" is the first Disney animated feature to return to theatres after release on video cassette. Disney wants to know what impact the videos will have on the box-office performance of the film, which grossed $26.5 million in its last theatrical run during the 1984 holiday season. Will the "Pinocchio" videos diminish the public's willingness to pay box-office prices in 1992?

A number of Disney analysts believe not. For starters, only 700,000 units of "Pinocchio" were sold in the 1985-1986 period, in contrast with the 14.2 **million** copies of "Fantasia" purchased last winter.

The "Pinocchio" videocassettes went out "before the marketplace really got developed," said Lisbeth R. Barron, an analyst with S.G. Warburg & Co. in New York. "I don't think this is a true test."

Still, "Pinocchio" illustrates the shrewd way Disney continues to exploit its animated franchise, which probably contributes the lion's share of earnings for Disney's filmed entertainment segment year in, year out.

No audience appreciates the Disney animated films more than Wall Street. With production costs already recouped, the older films quickly turn a profit. Even their marketing costs are lower, because the public already knows the title and storyline for classics such as "Cinderella" and "Sleeping Beauty."

And when the classics are sold as videos, Disney keeps an estimated 60% of the wholesale price as profit, providing a phenomenal boost to the company's earnings. Since Disney controls the timing of the classic films' release on video, it "helps them smooth earnings, whereas [other] films are always unpredictable," Barron said.

Disney has managed to show a steady increase in its filmed entertainment operating income for each year since the Michael Eisner-led management team took charge. Beginning in 1985 with $33.6 million, the unit's operating income rose to $318.1 million for the year ended Sept. 30, 1991.

Disney also expects to benefit from the good will built up with audiences from its more recent animated hits, "Little Mermaid" and "Beauty and the Beast."

"What's happening is a real resurgence in animation as an art form," said Dick Cook, president of Disney's film distribution arum. "There is a true rekindling of interest. It's not just for kids anymore."

Eisner, the Disney chairman, went even further: "I think that [the] film release of "Pinocchio" will be substantially higher than what we did in '84-'85 because of the interest in animation and the videos, which [are] really no more than advertising for their movies."

Cynics might turn Eisner's statement around, since the theatrical re-release of "101 Dalmatians" last summer clearly paved the way for the more profitable release of the film on video this spring. With 11 million cassettes shipped, Disney's revenue from home video (an estimated $150 million) far exceeded its share (about $32 million) of the film's box-office revenue.

Still, Eisner said the company hasn't decided whether it will re-release "Pinocchio" on video next year. "There's an emotional issue here. We want to make sure that we still have a library where parents want to go out and have a shared experience with their children in the theatre."

And Disney, for now has the luxury of keeping such money-makers off the market. With the production of "Little Mermaid," "Beauty and Beast" and other new animated films, Disney is stretching out the re-release of older films to nine or 10 years, as opposed to the traditional seven year rotation. In Europe, Disney has already adopted a 10-year cycle for the re-release of its animated classics.

So much, then for the criticism that Eisner and his people would plunder the Disney library. "Lady and the Tramp," which sold 3.5 million videos in 1987, may not be back in the theaters until 1995. By then, Disney is banking on normal wear-and-tear on the tapes, and a new generation of children or new parents shelling out at the box office window.

Teams

Agree not to cheat on the assignment. So, don't look at the graph on the backside of this page until you have finished question 1.

In Panamint Valley, California there is only one gas station for fifty miles. Your group owns the station.

1. What price would you charge? (It costs you $1.50 per gallon to get the gas, which is trucked in a long distance.)

    A. lowest price you would suggest: _____

    B. highest price you would suggest: _____

    C. a middle price: _____

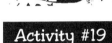

The Only Gas Station in Pana- mint Valley

2. Now look at the graph on the reverse side. What was the quantity demanded at each of your suggested prices?

Price	Qd
$____	____
$____	____
$____	____

3. Complete the following table for your suggested price:

Price	Qd	Total Revenue	Total Cost	Total Profit
$___	____	_____	_____	_____
$___	____	_____	_____	_____
$___	____	_____	_____	_____

4. Given the graph on the next page, can you do better? Pick a price that will maximize profits.

5. Explain why the Panamint Valley gas station will not gain more profit by charging a higher price.

6. Label the profit-maximizing Q. Graph ATC. (Hint: It will be a straight line.) Shade in TC, TR and profits.

continued

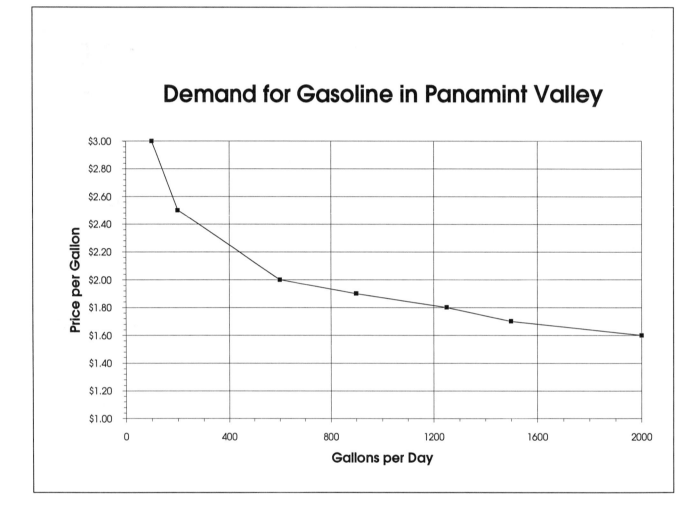

Demand for Gasoline in Panamint Valley

High Stakes -- a Game of Oligopoly

In this game, you will play one member of a firm in an oligopoly. An oligopoly is an industry dominated by a few firms. OPEC, the Organization of Petroleum Exporting Countries, for example, is made up of 14 nations. The U.S. domestic auto industry is dominated by three firms--GM, Ford and Chrysler.

Your goal in this game is to make as much money as you can for your firm. In each round of play, you will decide to price your product at a high price of $4.00, or a low price of $3.00. The other members of the oligopoly can decide to follow each other's decision, or to act independently. When one business in an oligopoly sets the price, and the rest of the firms follow, it is called "price leadership."

Your **revenues** are your money from the sale of your product. If you sell 30 at $4.00, your revenues are $120.00. You have **fixed and variable costs** in producing your product. Your fixed costs do not vary with the amount you produce, and are $55.00 each round. Rent, taxes, etc., represent your fixed costs. Your variable costs are $1.00 per unit sold each round. Labor and raw materials are variable costs. If you sell $30 units, your total cost is $85.00 ($55 fixed and $30 variable).

You make a profit when your revenues from sales are greater than costs. If you made $120 in revenues, for example, and your total costs were $85.00, your profit would be $35.00.

The members of your oligopoly may decide to compete with one another, or to agree on prices. **A warning however!** There can be no verbal agreements on prices.

To start, one member of your oligopoly will go first and indicate by hand signal if he/she is going to price high or low. The other two members privately record their price decisions. Then you'll figure out how you did.

Good luck.

continued

Pricing-Profit Situations (Oligopoly)

Industry			Individual Firm			
Prices (Firm Sales)	Total Sales	Price	Sales Quantity	Total Revenue P x Q	Total Cost $55 Fixed $1/Variable	Profit
H,H,H 30,30,30	90	H = $4				
H,H,L 10,10,80	100	H = $4				
		L = $3				
H,L,L 5,50,50	105	H = $4				
		L = $3				
L,L,L 36,36,36	108	L = $3				

Profit or Loss Statement

(Read the results from the prepared chart as you play)

No.	Industry Situation	Your Firm's Price (H or L)	Profit	Loss
1				
2				
3				
4				
5				
6				
7				
8				
9				
10				
11				
12				
13				
14				
15				
		Column Totals >	[ ]	[ ]
		Net Profit or Loss >		[ ]

Teams

After reading the *Wall Street Journal* article, "From Air to Pump to Puma's Disc System, Sneaker Gimmicks Bound to New Heights," on the next page, reach a consensus on the following statements. Are they true or false? Why?

1. The athletic shoe market is an example of a monopolistic competitive market, not an oligopoly market.

2. The two largest firms have 50% market share.

3. Puma came out with a disc system to differentiate its share from Nike and Reebok. With a unique product, they will earn economic profits.

4. Consumers buy Nike and Reebok shoes because they advertise more than others, not because they are better shoes.

5. Entry of new, more technologically sophisticated substitute shoes will reduce Nike's economic profits.

6. Adidas is choosing to engage in product differentiation.

7. Now complete the graph on the far right.

Sneaker Gimmicks

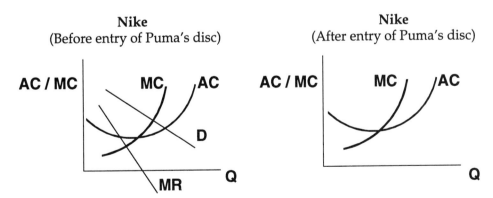

Nike
(Before entry of Puma's disc)

Nike
(After entry of Puma's disc)

What happens to price after entry into the market by Puma?

What happens to profits after entry of Puma?

continued

© Keenan & Maier

From Air to Pump to Puma's Disc System, Sneaker Gimmicks Bound to New Heights

By Joseph Pereira, Staff Reporter, *Wall Street Journal*, October 31, 1991

First came Nike's Air shoe. Then came Reebok's Pump. And now there's Puma's Disc System sneaker.

Forget about shoe laces and a tongue. The Disc System instead features a "Closure unit" that is turned like the dial on a ski boot, and "anatomically premolded compression unit" that replaces the tongue and "lateral stabilizing elements" that tighten the sides for a better fit. All for just $125 a pair.

It may sound more like astronaut gear than a sneaker, but that's the point. In the athletic footwear world, the race is not so much to the swift nowadays as to the one with the latest gimmick.

"This industry has turned into the battle of the bells and whistles...For a time, there even was a real wild shoe you could hook up to your computer to tell how far you've run," says Steven Frankel, an analyst at Adams Harkness & Hill Inc.

SLOW GROWING MARKET

Indeed, with the $5.5 billion U.S. sneaker market maturing and showing little growth, dozens of makers are touting their own high-technology shoes, from Adidas AG's Tortion Bar to Interco Inc.'s Converse Y-Bar to Hyde Inc.'s Saucony Ground Reaction Inertia Device to Reebok International Ltd.'s Avia Compression Chamber System.

Whether the Disc System Show will revive the sluggish sales of Puma USA, the U.S. unit of Sweden's Aritmos, remains to be seen. Most hot shoes have proved to be fads, as fickle buyers--especially teenagers, the biggest part of the market--switch brands frequently.

Reebok's Pump, which quickly became a big hit when it was introduced two years ago, already shows signs of being winded. So Reebok will soon introduce the Double Pump, a sneaker that---yes--features not one but two air bladders and two inflation gadgets to pump more air into more parts of the show. It will retail for $159 a pair.

PUMP'S FICKLE CUSTOMERS

The brief history of the Pump shows how tough the athletic shoe business has become--even for hits. Hoping to improve Reebok's image as a performance shoe, the company targeted the 18-to-35-year-old male. But most buyers were younger, as the shoe became a status symbol for teenagers and their pre-teen siblings. "I have four-year-olds coming into the store asking for the Pump," notes Liz Butler, assistant manager for Lady's Athlete's Food in Burlington, Mass. "And a friend of mine has an infant who wears pumps."

This year, the Pump will account for about 7% of Reebok's shoe sales. Reebok says it remains a strong brand, but orders have dropped, in part because kids are looking for something new. "It's a a very fickle, very fashion-oriented crowd," explains Josie Esquivel, a Shearson Lehman Brothers analyst. "With them, once the fizz is gone, that's it."

To be sure, the Pump was a breath of fresh air for Reebok, which two years ago lost the industry lead in sales to archrival Nike. The new line helped Reebok regain brand momentum, boost profits, hoist its stock price 250% this year and take a run at Nike. Stealing business from some of its smaller competitors, including L.A. Gear Inc., Reebok expanded its market share from 22% to 24%, much of the gain coming in the last year. That compares with Nike's 30%.

Backed by award-winning advertising, Nike's nine-year-old Air line is clearly the dominant brand in the market. In fiscal 1991, Nike sold 40 million pairs of its Air line. By comparison, Reebok sold six million pair of Pumps, albeit a much newer line, in two years.

Adidas, in fact is trying to take advantage of the confusion. To raise its shoes above the clutter, Adidas says in its current catalog, "People are tired of gimmicks, hype and inflated pricing. They want honest performance, quality and value...It's time to get back to what is essential."

Puma insists that its Disc System isn't a gimmick, but a major step forward in improving fit and performance. "Sure, a lot of us feel there are lots of gimmicks out there, but the Disc is giving consumers a tangible benefit," says John O'Rourke, president of Puma USA.

No matter how good the shoe is, it won't be easy for Puma to succeed against the marketing clout of Nike and Reebok, which dominate the market and spend more than $75 million a year each on advertising.

"There's so much product out there," says Jennifer Black Groves, analyst for Black and Co., in Portland, Ore., "Sometimes it comes down to who can shout the loudest and longest."

Teams

Allocate the following industries among your team members. In each case, calculate the concentration ratio and Herfindahl-Hirschman Index (HHI).

Industries and per cent of market share

Airlines

American 18%
United 17%
Delta 16%
Northwest 11%
Continental 9%

Concentration Ratio _____
HHI _____

Aspirin

Bayer 18%
Excedrin 18%
Bufferin 11%
Anacin 8%

Concentration Ratio _____
HHI _____

Auto Insurance

Allstate 11%
State Farm 9%
Farmers 5%
Nationwide 4%
Aetna 3%

Concentration Ratio _____
HHI _____

Breakfast Cereals

Kelloggs 42%
General Mills 18%
General Foods 16%

Concentration Ratio _____
HHI _____

Fast Food

McDonalds 20%
Burger King 9%
Wendy's 5%
Kentucky Fried Chick.. 5%
Hardees 4%
Pizza Hut 4%

Concentration Ratio _____
HHI _____

Quick Lube

Jiffy Lube 26%
Minute Lube 8%
Auto Spa 6%
Valvoline 5%
Grease Monkey 4%
Econo Lube 3%
Avis 2%

Concentration Ratio _____
HHI _____

Soft Drinks (International)

Coca Cola 33%
Pepsi 10%
Fanta 7%
Sprite 5%
Seven Up 2%

Concentration Ratio _____
HHI _____

Movies

Warner Brothers 17%
Universal 17%
Columbia 16%
Disney 14%
Paramount 14%
Orion 6%
Fox 6%
MGM/UA 6%

Concentration Ratio _____
HHI _____

Tires

Michelsen/Uniroyal/
    Goodrich 22%
Goodyear 18%
Bridgestone/Firestone 17%
Sumitomo/Dunlop 8%
Pirelli/Armstrong 7%
Continental/Genera 7%
Yokohama 4%

Concentration Ratio _____
HHI _____

Potato Chips

Frito Lay 38%
Borden 15%
Proctor & Gamble 9%

Concentration Ratio _____
HHI _____

Pet Food

Ralston Purina 27%
Nestles 12%
Mars 8%
Heinz 8%
Grand Metropolitan 7%
Quaker 7%

Concentration Ratio _____
HHI _____

Toilet Paper

Scott Paper 20%
James River 18%
Fort Howard.............. 16%
Proctor & Gamble 14%
Georgia Pacific 9%
Kimberley Clark 9%

Concentration Ratio _____
HHI _____

Music

Time Warner 30%
CBS/Sony 24%
Bertelsnian/RCA 19%
Polygram 16%
Thorn/EMI 7%
Matsushita/MCA 5%

Concentration Ratio _____
HHI _____

Soft Drinks (U.S.)

Coca Cola 40%
Pepsi 30%
Dr. Pepper 5%
Seven Up 5%

Concentration Ratio _____
HHI _____

How much market share does McDonald's have?

Teams

Answer the following questions. Be ready to report your results to the class.

1. Based on the concentration ratio, which industries are highly concentrated?

2. Based on the HHI, which industries are highly concentrated?

3. Which measure is more accurate, the concentration ratio or the HHI?

4. In the fast food industry, Kentucky Fried Chicken and Pizza Hut were both bought by Pepsico. How would this ownership change the HHI?

5. The U.S. Justice Department is likely to challenge any merger between two firms if the HHI is already above 1800 and the merger raises the index by at least 100. Would the Justice Department likely approve a merger of Kelloggs and General Mills?

'Kinky' Demand

Teams

You and your teammates manufacture and sell light bulbs. It is a lucrative market with only a few competitors. Nonetheless, you watch your competitor's prices carefully. Whenever another firm lowers prices, you match it; whenever another firm raises prices, you maintain your lower price in order to gain market share. Use the graph on the following page to find the profit-maximizing output and price level for your light bulbs.

Step 1 Profit-maximizing
• On the graph, label the marginal revenue line, the demand curve and the marginal cost line. Find the profit-maximizing level of output for this firm.
• Check with your teammates, to make certain that you have correctly identified each line and the profit-maximizing level of output.

Step 2 Falling costs
The cost of glass falls slightly. What will happen to your MC curve? Draw a new MC curve for these slightly lower costs. What happens to profit-maximizing output and prices?

Step 3 Kinked demand curve
Cut or tear this page along the dotted lines. Take care not to cut or tear too far. Then slide the bottom right-hand corner of the sheet under the bottom left-hand side of the sheet until points A and B line up.

• You should see a "kink" develop in your price line and a blank space appear in your MR line.

• Is there a clear-cut price at which MR = MC? Check your answer with your teammates.

Step 4 Why a kink?
At the start, all light bulb manufacturers sell at the price of $1 per light bulb. When you made the kink, you made the demand curve become steeper at lower prices. Is the demand curve is more or less elastic at lower prices?

Explain why this will be true in the light bulb market.

Above the price of $1, is the kinked demand curve more or less elastic? Explain why this will be true in the light bulb market.

What is the best price strategy for your firm?

continued

Step 5 Consequences of the kink

Notice that the kinked demand curve causes a gap in the marginal revenue curve. When you cut costs, causing the MC to fall, was there a change in profit-maximizing output? Check your answer with your teammates.

How was your response to lower costs different before you introduced the kink?

As a consumer, what is a disadvantage of buying a good or service in a market with a kinked demand curve?

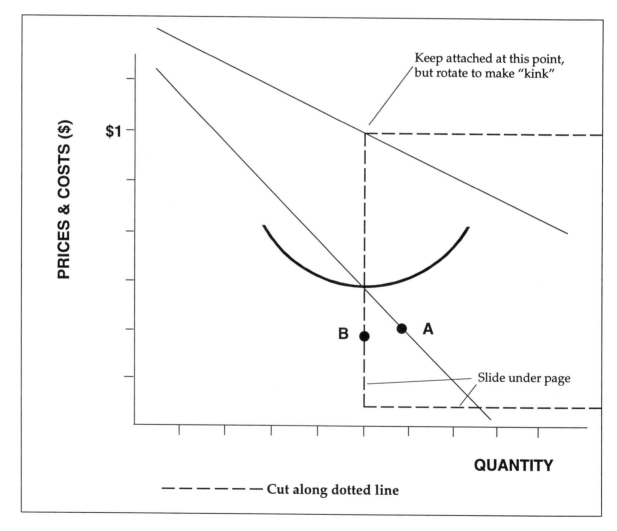

Keep attached at this point, but rotate to make "kink"

$1

PRICES & COSTS ($)

B   A

Slide under page

QUANTITY

— — — — — Cut along dotted line

Step 1

Read the *New York Times* article, "Stroh Brewing to Sell Major Brands to Coors", reprinted on the following page.

Step 2

• As instructed, find a partner. You and your partner will be assigned either the square or rounded-corner box below.

• Depending on your assignment, fill in the left side of the chart for either the square or rounded corner box.

Should Coors Beer be allowed to acquire Stroh?

Proposed: The U.S. Department of Justice should permit the acquisition of Stroh by Coors.

Pro arguments:	Other group's Con arguments:
1.	1.
2.	2.
3.	3.

Proposed: The U.S. Department of Justice should permit the acquisition of Stroh by Coors.

Con arguments:	Other group's Pro arguments:
1.	1.
2.	2.
3.	3.

continued

© Keenan & Maier

Step 3

"Pro" pair find a "Con" pair to make a group of four. Pro side reads 3 arguments to con side. Con side records. Then con side reads 3 arguments to pro side. Pro side records.

Step 4

Choose by consensus the best argument on each side.

Step 5

If you were the U.S. Department of Justice, would you permit this acquisition?

Stroh Brewing to Sell Major Brands to Coors
Deal Ends 200 Years of Family Ownership

By Michael Lev, *The New York Times*, September 25, 1983

The long-term trend toward consolidation in the American beer industry continued yesterday as the family-owned Stroh Brewing Company of Detroit agreed to sell most of its brands and breweries to the Adolf Coors Company for $425 million in cash and assumed debt.

Assuming the sale receives regulatory approvals, it could establish Coors as a third major player in an industry that has increasingly been dominated by two companies--Anheuser-Busch and Miller Brewing.

With the Stroh brands, Coors would have 18.7 percent of the American beer market compared with Anheuser-Busch, which as 42.8 percent, and Miller brewing with 21.8 percent, according to Merrill Lynch Capital Markets.

The merger of Coors, currently ranked fourth in the domestic beer market, and Stroh, ranked third was viewed by industry analysts and consultants as necessary for the survival of either company. Both have been losing market share to Anheuser-Busch, which has outpaced its rivals by spending heavily on marketing and advertising.

Stroh has had trouble riding out the slump in beer sales and announced earlier this year that it was seeking to sell a minority stake in the company. Then in May, the company announced that it was talking with Coors about a combination.

AN ESSENTIAL MOVE

"Anheuser-Busch and Miller have such a hold on the market that this was an essential move," said Tom Pirko, president of the Bevmark Corporation, a consulting company, of the merger.

"There were three companies there floundering around," Mr. Pirko said, referring to Stroh, Coors and G. Heilman Company, a regional brewer that is currently the nation's fifth largest.

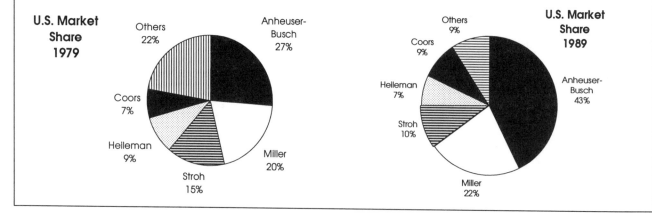

U.S. Market Share 1979: Others 22%, Anheuser-Busch 27%, Coors 7%, Heileman 9%, Stroh 15%, Miller 20%

U.S. Market Share 1989: Others 9%, Coors 9%, Heileman 7%, Stroh 10%, Anheuser-Busch 43%, Miller 22%

Finance

Reprinted below is a section of the daily summary for August 25, 1993 of the New York Stock Exchange.

1. Working on your own: Imagine you could go back in time to buy and sell any single stock sometime during the previous year. Based on the 52 week high and low prices for stocks, choose one stock that will earn you high capital gains.

This stock is: _____

The capital gain was:

2. Compare your choice with other members of the group. If you had $1,000 to invest, which one stock would be the best investment based on its capital gain. It is:

Explain how you made this choice.

3. Working on your own again, choose one stock that is a good investment based on the reported dividend.

This stock is:

_____

The dividend was:

Up & Down the Stock Market

Stock	365 Day High	Low	Dividend	Yield(%)
Abbtlab	33	22	.68	2.6
Avon	64	50	1.80	3.0
Bausch	59	43	.88	1.9
BlackD	22	14	.40	2.0
Boeing	41	33	1.00	2.5
Borden	29	14	.60	3.6
Caterp	83	46	.60	0.7
Chryslr	47	19	.60	1.4
ClubMd	27	18	.30	1.1
DeltaAL	61	45	.20	0.4
EKodak	61	39	2.00	3.2
Gap	38	27	.40	1.4
GM	49	28	.80	1.7
Kmart	28	19	.96	4.2
Kellogg	75	47	1.36	2.6
PepsiC	43	34	.64	1.7
Polaroid	38	25	.60	1.6
QuakerO	77	59	1.92	2.8
RalsPu	49	33	1.20	3.0
TimeW	40	22	.32	0.8
Wendys	15	11	.24	1.7
Zenix	8	6	.81	10.5

continued

4. Compare your choice with other members of the group. Decide which one stock would be the best investment based on its dividend.

It is:

Explain how you made this choice. *(Hint: you need to look at the "yield" column.)*

5. Pretend you are speaking with your 15 year old brother who is eager to invest in the stock market. Explain in your own words why the real stock market isn't as easy as the choices you made in steps 1 to 4 above.

6. Read your explanation to the other group members. Write a better explanation using the ideas of others in the group.

Teams

In this game your group will decide on the tax rates for the country of Taxhaven. It is necessary for you to collect $1,000 billion in taxes. You will have three taxes to choose from:

1. Personal income tax   **2. Sales tax**   **3. Payroll tax**

Step 1

Count off 1,2,3,1,2,3, and so on.

All number 1's will work on the personal income tax; number 2's will work on the sales tax; number 3's will work on the payroll tax.

Group 1: Personal income tax

You must decide on the personal income tax for three income groups: lower, middle, and upper income. For each group you will choose the marginal tax rate.

The marginal tax rate means:

> *For reference, the marginal tax rates for a married couple household in the U.S. in 1993 were 15% for income below about $40,000 , 28% for income over about $40,000, and up to nearly 40% for income above $250,000.*

Your choices are: 0%; 5%; 10%; 15%; 20%; 25%; 30%; 35%; 40%; 45%; or 50%.

Lower (under $40,000) _____   Middle ($40,000-$100,000) _____

Upper (over $100,000) _____

In the table below find how much revenue you will collect from each group.

Total Revenue: **Lower $ _____ + Middle $ _____ + Upper $ _____ = $ _____ billion**

Income tax revenue (in billions of $) at Various Tax Rates											
	0%	5%	10%	15%	20%	25%	30%	35%	40%	45%	50%
Lower	$0	$25	$50	$75	$100	$125	$150	$175	$200	$225	$250
Middle	$0	$50	$100	$150	$200	$250	$300	$350	$400	$450	$500
Upper	$0	$20	$40	$60	$80	$100	$120	$140	$160	$180	$200

Now rejoin the rest of the group.

The
Tax
Game

continued

Economics
LIVE / 45

Group 2: Sales tax

You must decide the sales tax for the country of Bliss. For reference, what is the sales tax in your community? _____%

The sales tax in Taxhaven will be _____%

Look up the revenue generated by this tax in the table below. It is: $_____billion.

Sales Tax Revenue (in billions of $) at Various Sales Tax Rates							
	0%	2%	4%	6%	8%	10%	12%
Revenue	$0	$60	$120	$180	$240	$300	$360

Now rejoin the rest of the group.

Group 3: Payroll tax

In the country of Bliss the payroll tax is similar to the U.S. social security tax system. It is collected at a flat rate on almost all earnings up to $60,000 per year. After this amount the payroll tax is collected at a much lower rate. For reference it is approximately 8% in the U.S., with a similar percentage paid by the employer.

The employee payroll tax in Bliss will be _____%.

Look up the revenue generated by this tax in the tables. It is: $ _____ billion.

Payroll Tax Revenue (in billions of $) at Various Tax Rates							
	0%	2%	4%	6%	8%	10%	12%
Revenue	$0	$75	$150	$225	$300	$375	$450

Now rejoin the rest of the group.

Step 2

Bring the groups back together and report how much you collected from each tax:

1. From income tax $ _____billion

2. From sales tax $ _____billion

3. From payroll tax $ _____billion

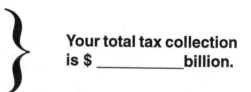

Your total tax collection is $ _____billion.

If it is less than $1,000 billion you need to raise at least one of your taxes. Decide together which tax or taxes you will increase, making certain that the new rate will collect at least $1,000 billion (Don't worry if you are a little bit over.)

If your tax collection is more than $1,100 billion, then you need to lower at least one of your taxes. Decide together which tax or taxes you will decrease.

When your total tax collection is at least $1,000 billion **and** less than $1,100, go on to the next step.

Step 3

You will now measure the effect of your taxes on different income groups. *This is called the tax incidence.* It differs from the tax rates because not all income is taxed. There are tax deductions for the income tax, untaxed items for the sales tax and income untaxed for the payroll tax.

Income Tax Incidence Table:

Income Tax Rate	0%	5%	10%	15%	20%	25%	30%	35%	40%	45%	50%
					(Circle your three rates)						
Tax Incidence for Lower Income Group	0%	2%	5%	8%	10%	13%	15%	18%	20%	23%	25%
Tax Incidence for Middle Income Group	0%	2%	5%	8%	10%	13%	15%	18%	20%	23%	25%
Tax Incidence for High Income Group	0%	2%	5%	8%	10%	13%	15%	18%	20%	23%	25%

Sales Tax Incidence Table:

Sales Tax Rate	0%	2%	4%	6%	8%	10%	12%
			(Circle your three rates)				
Tax Incidence for Lower Income Group	0%	1%	3%	4%	6%	8%	10%
Tax Incidence for Middle Income Group	0%	1%	2%	2%	3%	4%	5%
Tax Incidence for High Income Group	0%	0%	1%	1%	2%	2%	3%

Payroll Tax Incidence Table:

Payroll Tax Rate	0%	2%	4%	6%	8%	10%	12%
			(Circle your three rates)				
Tax Incidence for Lower Income Group	0%	3%	6%	9%	11%	14%	18%
Tax Incidence for Middle Income Group	0%	2%	4%	6%	9%	12%	15%
Tax Incidence for High Income Group	0%	1%	3%	5%	6%	7%	9%

Effect on the **lower** income group: Income tax incidence _____% + Sales tax incidence _____% + Payroll tax incidence _____% = _____%

Effect on the **middle** income group : Income tax incidence _____% + Sales tax incidence _____% + Payroll tax incidence _____% = _____%

Effect on the **high** income group : Income tax incidence _____% + Sales tax incidence _____% + Payroll tax incidence _____% = _____%

Questions

1. Is your overall tax system progressive or regressive? Why?

2. Which tax tended to make your system progressive?

3. Which tax tended to make your system regressive?

4. To improve the tax incidence, go back to step 1. Adjust your income, sales and payroll tax rates so that you are satisfied with the effect on each income group.

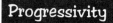

Soak the Rich?

Teams

The U.S. Federal personal income tax is a progressive tax--tax rates increase at higher incomes. During the early 1980s, the top marginal tax bracket was reduced from 49% to 28%. Since then, it has been increased. In this exercise you will debate the 1993 increase to nearly 40% for households with taxable over $250,000.

Your pair will be assigned one of the shapes below (square or curved):

Proposed: The marginal tax rate should be raised from 31% to 40% for households with taxable income of more than $250,000 per year.

Pro arguments:	Other group's Con arguments:
1.	1.
2.	2.
3.	3.

Proposed: The marginal tax rate should be raised from 31% to 40% for households with taxable income of more than $250,000 per year.

Con arguments:	Other group's Pro arguments:
1.	1.
2.	2.
3.	3.

Step 1

"Pro" pair find a "Con" pair to make a group of four. Pro side reads 3 arguments to con side. Con side records. Then con side reads 3 arguments to pro side. Pro side records.

Step 2

Choose by consensus the best argument on each side.

Your instructor has polled your class about household incomes. The cumulative percentage of households and cumulative percentage of income are:

	% of total households	Income received	% of total income
Lowest 5	____%	$_____	____%
Lowest 10	____%	$_____	____%
Lowest 15	____%	$_____	____%
Lowest 20	____%	$_____	____%
Lowest 25	____%	$_____	____%
•			
•			
•			
continue until			
Total Class Income	100%	$_____	100%

Income inequality

Teams

Step 1

Based on the numbers above, draw the Lorenz curve for the class on the graph below.

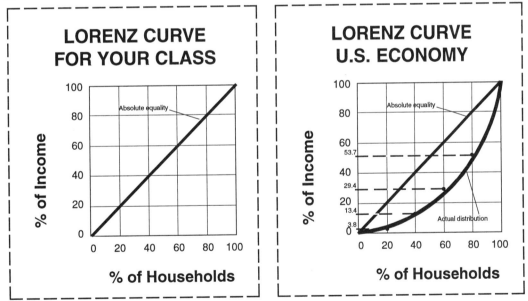

© Keenan & Maier

Step 2

1. Is income distributed more or less equally among households in your class than in the U.S. as a whole? Explain.

2. The Gini coefficient is the area between the diagonal and the Lorenz Curve divided by the area below the diagonal. For the U.S. it is about 0.43. Calculate the Gini Coefficient for your class by counting the squares between the diagonal and your class Lorenz Curve. Estimate partial squares as 1/8, 1/4 and so on. Divide this number by the number of squares below the diagonal--it will be 12.5.

- -

Confidential survey--do not put your name on this section.

During the previous year, the total pre-tax income in my household was approximately:

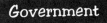

Teams

The table below shows the 1993-1994 proposed U.S. Federal budget (in billions).

1. Social security	$321	8. Veterans	$38
2. Defense	$277	9. Environment	$21
3. Health	$265	10. International affairs	$19
4. Income security	$215	11. Science	$18
5. Net interest	$212	12. Agriculture	$17
6. Education	$54	Other	$56
7. Transportation	$40		

Total Spending	**$1553**
Projected Tax Revenue	**- $1200**

Estimated Deficit	**$353**

Uncle Sam's Budget

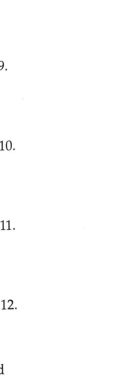

Step 1

Number off 1, 2, 3.... to 12. (Each person will have 2 or more numbers.) Beginning with person number one, give a specific example for each line in the budget. For example, person number one might list payments to the disabled as an example of social security payments. If you are stuck, consult with other members of the group. If no one can explain a line, star it to ask for help later.

1. (Payments to the disabled)
Fill in another example:

7.

2.

8.

3.

9.

4.

10.

5.

11.

6.

12.

continued

Step 2

Individually, decide on at least three changes that you would make in this budget. You may make any three changes you like, but the budget deficit must not be any greater than its current level of $353 billion.

My three proposed changes are:

	Line to be changed	Amount
1.		
2.		
3.		

Step 3

Read your proposed changes to your group members. You must now decide together on at least three changes that everyone can support. You will report this proposal to the class. If your group cannot reach a common decision, you must report the budget as it presently stands.

Group recommendation:

	Line to be changed	Amount
1.		
2.		
3.		

Economics has been influenced by three major philosophical traditions.

Step 1

List five ideas associated with each of the following economic traditions:

Classical   **Keynesian**   **Marxian**

Economic perspectives part 1

Step 2

1. How would you classify the article *"U.S. Sliding to Third World Status"*? Underline three phrases to support your position.

2. How would you classify the article *"Up in the Air?"* Underline three phrases to support your position.

3. How would you classify the article, *"Fixing the U.S. Economy?"* Underline three phrases to support your position.

Step 3

Brainstorm as a team to identify two pieces of evidence supporting the classical view that the U.S. economy is self-regulating itself toward full employment at the present time.

Brainstorm as a team to identify two pieces of evidence supporting the Keynesian or Marxian view that the U.S. economy is **not** self-regulating itself toward full employment at the present time.

continued

U.S. Sliding to Third World Status

by David M. Gordon
Los Angeles Times, September 8, 1991

In the current global context, several leading features seem to best characterize trends in less developed capitalist Third World economies. These economies tend to display:

- Dramatically increasing inequalities in income and wealth;
- Chronic foreign trade deficits (with heavy reliance on agricultural and raw materials exports);
- Stagnant productivity growth;
- Vast surplus pools of low-wage and relatively unskilled workers;
- The existence of a large underclass with few regular ties to the formal market economy;
- Relatively high rates of infant mortality, and
- If and where their political systems are formally democratic, phlegmatic or declining popular participation in their political processes.

We are, by all relevant standards, an advanced capitalist economy, one of the wealthiest and most powerful in the world. But the dominant trends in the U.S. economy during the past 10 years appear to have been moving us steadily in directions more reminiscent of backward economies.

Let's take the above list of seven features characteristic of less developed economies and examine the U.S. economy by each of those criteria in turn.

There is little debate about the prominence of the first trend: Inequalities in income and wealth have intensified dramatically in the United States since the mid-to late 1970s.

Nor is there much debate about the second trend. Since the late 1970s, we have had a chronic foreign trade deficit in the United States that steadfastly refused to disappear. And, echoing a kind of primary product trade dependence characteristic of developing economies, we would be in much more serious trouble, indeed, if it were not for our net trading surplus in our two major "cash crops"-agricultural products and military hardware.

To some degree, the third and fourth trends together. One of the most important sources of tepid productivity growth in the U.S. economy involves the relatively increasing reliance by U.S. companies on low-wage labor. Here, the comparison with Third World economies is particularly salient.

The fifth trend is particularly troubling. Like the residents of slums of Mexico City, Sao Paulo or Calcutta, those members of the "underclass" enduring ghetto life in many U.S. cities have been cut loose by the larger society, left to founder while the more affluent classes frolic.

The sixth trend especially tarnishes our image as the leader of the Western World. With rising relative poverty in many urban and rural areas, more and more infants in the United States are born into unhealthy environments. Infant mortality rates represent the tip of that iceberg. And there, by the late 1980s, we had fallen back to the relative levels of recently industrializing countries. In 1989, 15 countries, including all of our leading economic competitors, had lower infant mortality rates than the United States; we were tied with Greece and Spain, and we were barely ahead of Cuba.

Finally, more and more people choose to abstain from the U.S. political process. There are many explanations of trends toward declining citizen participation in elections.

One common and apparently plausible account links declining participation rates to the failure of the government and both major political parties in the United States to address the sources of eroding standards of living among vast portions of the population. This is equally an explanation that is often applied to many developing countries.

Can (these trends) be reversed? There are many steps we could take to begin to arrest our slide toward the profile of developing economies. But first we would need to decide that we care, that we actually wanted to reverse that slide.

It would appear that most of the wealthy and powerful in this country, as in many Third World countries, couldn't care less. How long should we continue to allow those who are sitting pretty to play such a dominant role in setting our national priorities?

Up in the Air

by Milton Friedman
Newsweek, July 28, 1969

This column was begun in a jet that had crossed the Atlantic in six hours but had now been circling Kennedy for an hour, stacked up awaiting permission to land.

What waste. A multimillion dollar jet, a marvel of modern technology manned by a highly skilled and highly paid crew, occupied by nearly 200 passengers, many spending highly valuable time, serviced by a pleasant and attractive complement of hostesses, guzzling fuel as it circled aimlessly high in the sky. The cost was easily thousands of dollars an hour.

How is it that this waste occurs, not only occasionally, which is no doubt unavoidable, but regularly, so that experienced travelers, let alone the airlines, regard it as a routine matter? How is it that the large financial return from eliminating the waste is not an effective prod?

Socialism vs. capitalism

As I sat in the plane, I reflected that the airplane manufacturers seem to be able to turn out these marvelous mechanical miracles in ample number to meet the demand of the airlines for them. The airlines seem to be able to acquire the highly skilled flight crews in ample number (with a real assist, it is true, from the military services, which train most of them). They seem to be able to hire sufficient stewardesses to woman the cabins. Occasionally, a plane is delayed by mechanical trouble, but the airlines generally have been able to acquire the skilled maintenance and ground men to service the planes, so this is seldom a bottleneck. I have heard no stories of planes being delayed by the inability of get ample airplane fuel, or meals to feed passengers, or liquor to befuddle them.

How it is that it has been possible to attend to all these matters--and yet not to arrange things on the ground, so that planes can generally be landed promptly and without delay? Is it somehow inherently more difficult to arrange space for landing planes than to build them and operate them in the air? That seems very dubious indeed.

I believe the answer to the puzzle is much simpler. Every other activity described is mostly private and highly competitive--private enterprise builds the planes, private (or where governmental, highly competitive) airlines fly them, private firms produce and supply the fuel for man and machine. The airports, on the other hand, are a socialized monopoly--financed and run by government. As a result, there is not effective way that the waste involved in airport delays can be converted into effective pressure to eliminate them. The pressure must make its convoluted way through the FAA, the Administration, Congress and local governments.

There is no reason why this need be so. In the heyday of free enterprise, the railroads built and almost wholly financed their own terminals--even when they were "union" terminals servicing a number of lines--and still operate them. Why should airlines not be required to provide their own landing facilities--not necessarily directly but perhaps by paying fees to other private enterprises that run the airports? The airlines doubtless initially welcomed Federal subsidization of landing facilities. I wonder whether they now think they really got a bargain?...

Too pat?

Many a reader will regard my explanation as too pat-- as simply a knee jerk reaction of an economic liberal(in the original sense of that much-abused term). Maybe so--but I urge them to see whether the shoe does not fit, not only here but elsewhere. Where are the long lines of frustrated drivers? At the doors of the automobile dealers selling cars produced by private enterprise--or on the highways and city streets provided by government? What are the problems plaguing education? A shortage of high-quality desks, chairs, and other educational equipment, including books, produced by private enterprise--or the inefficient organization and conduct of public schools? Where is technology backward and primitive? In the privately run telephone industry (albeit the existence of monopoly does occasionally produce delay and inefficiency)--or in the governmentally run Post Office?

Fixing the U.S. Economy

Signed by Nobel laureates: Kenneth Arrow, Lawrence R. Klein, Franco Modigliani, William Sharpe, Robert Solow, James Tobin and more than 50 other economists. *Challenge*, March 1992

The U.S. economy faces both a short-run problem and a long-run problem. The two are quite different. For the immediate future the problem is temporary shortage of demand. For the longer run the prospect is slow growth of productivity and therefore slow growth of incomes, more and more unequally distributed between the best and worst off. Everyone agrees that the remedy for the long-run problem is more investment: in people, in infrastructure, in technology, and in machinery.

Long before the recession wages had been falling behind inflation, far behind the aspirations of American workers. It is tempting to try to compensate for these disappointments by lowering taxes. But this is counter-productive. The only long-run solution is to raise the growth of productivity. Wages will follow. A far better vehicle for immediate stimulus is a program of federal assistance to state and local governments, aimed at increasing public investment in all forms, including education, which has suffered severely just at a time when improved and expanded education is widely recognized as an essential key to the future productivity and competitiveness of Americans.

We believe, therefore, that the Congress should enact and the President should sign a program of additional federal assistance to state and local governments amounting to at least $50 billion a year (about 1 percent of GDP). The spending of these funds will help to stimulate the economy. Since the economy has idle resources of labor and capital available to meet additional spending with additional production and the threat of inflation is minimal, it is appropriate to let these expenditures add to the deficit financed by borrowing, and it would cancel most or all of the needed stimulus to aggregate demand if they were financed otherwise.

The long run problems of our economy will not be solved in a year or two. The provision of federal aid to state and local governments should be part of a continuing long-run program. In later years, more elaborate targeting could be developed, to insure that the assistance is directed toward investment in people, knowledge, and productive infrastructure. Once the economy has substantially recovered, it will no longer be appropriate to pay for the program by federal borrowing. Instead, we propose that Congress and the President plan now to finance it by a combination of future cuts in defense spending and higher taxes.

The nation cannot afford the economic waste and human distress of protracted high unemployment. We can put America back to work, and we can do it in ways that will enable our workers to be more and more productive in years to come.

Teams

On the following page are six quotes by famous economists. After the exercise is complete, your instructor will identify the author of each quote. Your assignment is to identify what perspective each quote represents: is the author a classical (or conservative), a Keynesian (or liberal) or a Marxist (or radical)?

Number off 1,2,3,4,5,6.

    Person # 1: read the first quote. Other group members, listen carefully for phrases that identify the perspective of the author. Underline these phrases on your copy of the quote.

    Entire group: What is the perspective of the quote? _____ Make certain that everyone agrees and can explain why the quote is representative of this perspective.

    Person # 2: read the second quote. Other group members listen carefully for phrases that identify the perspective of the author. Underline these phrases on your copy of the quote.

    Entire group: What is the perspective of the quote? _____ Make certain that everyone agrees and can explain why the quote is representative of this perspective.

Continue process for:

Quote # 3:

Quote # 4:

Quote # 5:

Quote # 6:

Economic perspectives part 2

continued

1. "The very same arguments that for two centuries supported the ceding of political choice to the mass of people rather than its retention by a single individual or a small group, also provide the rationale for production and investment decision making by workers and consumers, not by individual capital owners or their managers."

2. "The United States has continued to progress; its citizens have become better fed, better clothed, better housed, and better transported; class and social distinctions have narrowed; minority groups have become less disadvantaged; popular culture has advanced by leaps and bounds. All this has been the product of the initiative and drive of individuals cooperating through the free market. Government measures have hampered not helped this development."

3. "Over the years, society has found it necessary to treat the blemishes of real-world private enterprise in many ways--regulation and consumer information to guard against the nefarious or careless producer... (Yet) judged purely as a system of productive efficiency, contemporary American capitalism has to get a high grade. It needs a tune-up, and perhaps even an overhaul, but not a trade-in."

4. "The remarkable flexibility of the U.S. economy which stems from its reliance on free markets, is a major national asset... Government regulation generally serves to reduce economic flexibility and thus should have a very limited role. Where regulation is necessary, regulatory programs should pass strict cost-benefit tests and should seek to harness the power of market forces to serve the public interest, not to distort or diminish those forces."

5. "We do not have to accept the dismal cycle of inflation and slump, a cycle which spells economic ruin and misery for people and for business.. It is not beyond our political and economic wit to do better than we have been doing, to attain a condition that represents something close to what economists call "full employment," and to do it with nearly stable prices."

6. "The economics of greed has reigned long enough. It is time to propel the economy in a more rational and democratic direction. It is time for a real change in the way we run our economy. We are committed to an economics that will offer sustainable improvements in living standards, strong democracy and community at home and global cooperation abroad, and more extensive economic fairness."

Teams

After conducting the Confidential Unemployment Survey on the other side of this page, your instructor will give you the data to complete Step 1.

Step 1

1. Number in survey: _____

2. Number reporting at least one hour per week of paid employment: _____

3. Number working ≤ 34 hours = _____ ; ≥ 35 hours = _____

4. Number not working, but actively seeking work: _____

5. Number not working and not seeking work who are:

    students _____   homemakers _____   none of the above _____

    retired _____   institutionalized _____

Step 2

Count off in your group 1 through 9. (Each person will have more than one number.) Person #1 answers question #1, person #2 answers question #2, and so on.

Calculate the following:

    1. The number of employed is:

    2. The number of unemployed is:

    3. The labor force is (#1 plus #2):

    4. The unemployment rate is:

    5. The percentage of part-time workers is (those working less than 35 hours per week):

What is the Unemployment Rate?

continued

6. Why might an individual have represented himself or herself as unemployed when in fact that individual is employed?

7. Why might an individual be counted as "not in the labor force" when that person might actually want a job?

8. Why might an individual be counted as employed, but not be working as many hours as he or she wishes?

9. Classify the individuals in questions 6, 7 and 8 as: discouraged workers, under-employed or phantom unemployed.

Confidential Unemployment Survey:

1. Did you work last week for pay (not including school or work around the house)?

☐ Yes   ☐ No

If yes, how many hours _____ (If yes, end of survey; if no continue.)

2. Did you look for work during the last four weeks through a specific activity such as applying to an employer?

☐ Yes   ☐ No   (If yes, end of survey; if no, continue.)

3. What did you do most during the last week?

☐ Student   ☐ Homemaker   ☐ Retired

☐ In an institution ☐ None of the above

Teams

Classify the following examples as structural, frictional, seasonal or cyclical unemployment—or **not** unemployed.

Make sure everyone agrees before going on to the next item.

	STRUCTURAL	FRICTIONAL	SEASONAL	CYCLICAL

1. Cheryl Ladd just finished her last movie and is looking for her next film.

2. Tim Tromer was laid off from his construction job because of the recession.

3. Jennifer Waxem just graduated from college and is searching for her first job.

4. Tom Hyde quit his oil exploration job with a U.S. company in Saudi Arabia and is searching for work in Connecticut.

5. Kim Lee has been laid off from the Aerospace Corporation because of defense cutbacks.

6. Tom Johnson is retiring voluntarily from the Navy and is looking for work in Los Angeles.

7. Keree Knell has been laid off from Security Pacific Bank because of its merger with Bank of America.

8. Armando Valdez has been laid off by IBM as part of the company's cost-cutting move.

9. Linda Bernette is taking voluntary retirement from teaching and is looking for part-time work.

10. Soo Li, a homemaker of 20 years, is out looking for her first paid job.

11. Roger the Dodger, a gang member and drug dealer, is working and earning big bucks.

12. Isabel Morada was laid off from her job at Apple Computer and the only work she could find was in fast food restaurants. She is not now looking for work.

13. Sarah Lorey has quit her job to stay home and raise her first child.

14. Christi Sims has been laid off from Macy's Department Store because of declining sales.

15. The six year-old California drought reduced the demand for fruit processors and ski instructors.

Classifying the Unemployed

Teams

You will be given a card by your instructor listing one type of unemployment.

Make sure everyone in your group understands the definition of this type of unemployment.

> Now, prepare a short one or two minute skit for the rest of the class illustrating this type of unemployment *without using the name on the card*. Include all group members in the skit.

Step 1

Consumer Price Index

Teams

As a group, choose four products that you buy regularly. Then agree on the prices of those products *last* year, and how many on average you bought last year. Then agree on the price this year.

Product	Price last year	Quantity bought last year	Price now
1.			
2.			
3.			
4.			

Step 2

To calculate a simplified CPI using last year as the base year:

$$CPI = \frac{\Sigma \ p_i \times q_o}{\Sigma \ p_o \times q_o} \times 100$$

Σ = sum of
p_o = prices in the base year
q_o = quantity in base year
p_i = prices now

The price index for now is =

The price index for the base year =

The rate of inflation =

How does the Bureau of Labor Statistics measurement of inflation differ from your simplified survey?

Activity #35

Your own CPI

Teams

The actual CPI uses percentages of income spent on various categories of purchases--housing, clothing, food and so on--to represent the quantities. These percentages are based on a survey of households.

Step 1
Conduct a simplified survey of your team. How much of your team's yearly spending goes to:

Education	Clothing	Medical Care	Transportation	All other
_____% +	_____% +	_____% +	_____% +	_____% = **100%**

(note that these *must* total 100%)

Step 2
Calculate your own CPI by multiplying the contribution to inflation of each product by multiplying your percentage spent in each area times the price index for that product area.

Your spending on:		Inflation index		
education _____%	x	200	=	_____
clothing _____%	x	130	=	_____
medical care _____%	x	200	=	_____
transportation _____%	x	130	=	_____
all other _____%	x	150	=	_____
			Total	_____

This number should total somewhere between 130 and 200. (Make sure you put the decimal place in the right location.)   **The CPI currently is about 150.**

1. How does your CPI compare with the current CPI? If it is more than 150 then you are affected by inflation more than the typical urban consumer; if it less than 150 then you are affected by inflation less than the typical urban consumer.

2. Why were you affected more or less by inflation than the typical urban consumer?

3. Which product area *most* affected your inflation rate?

Your instructor will conduct an auction during class. Keep track of quantities and prices:

Round 1		Round 2	
Quantity	Price sold	Quantity	Price sold
$\Sigma\, Q_1 \times P_1$ Round 1 = _____		$\Sigma\, Q_2 \times P_2$ Round 2 = _____	

$$CPI_{\text{for Round 2}} = \frac{\Sigma\ Q_2 \times P_2}{\Sigma\ Q_1 \times P_1} \times 100 = \underline{\hspace{1.5cm}}$$

An Inflationary Auction

Teams
Answer the following:

1. On average items priced $1.00 in the base period (round 1), in round 2 cost
$ _____ .

2. The rate of inflation during the auction was _____%.

3. What was the cause of inflation during the auction?

continued

Economics
LIVE / 65

4. Why were the quantities of goods sold held constant in both rounds?

5. If this rate of inflation persisted, what would happen to people's wage demands?

   • What would happen to costs of production?

6. Who would be hurt by inflation?

   • Who would benefit?

7. During the auction was there demand-pull inflation or cost-push inflation? Why?

8. (optional) Using AD/AS curves, describe the inflation during the auction.

Hyperinflation---inflation over 1000% per month--often accompanies war. The 1993 civil war in the former Yugoslavia is a case in point. Production in Serbia was ravaged by war and exacerbated by U.N. economic sanctions and a government that paid its bills by printing money.

Teams

Divide your team into 3 parts. Each group will read the following items, looking for:

Group 1-- Items that cause a change in aggregate demand

Group 2-- Items that cause a change in aggregate supply

Group 3-- Items that are consequence of hyperinflation

Inflation at 10 billion % a year?

From *"Currency Crisis Takes Toll on Serb Spirits,"*
Los Angeles Times, July, 1993.

1. Serbian prices rose 350% in one week during 1993.

2. The Serbian government printed money to pay farmers for the wheat they have raised.

3. In one hour the Dinar (Serbian currency) went from 1 U.S. dollar = 1,450,000 Dinars to 1 U.S. dollar = 2,030,000 Dinars.

4. The Serb government is paying for two years of war by printing money.

5. The latest estimate of the inflation rate is 10 billion percent a year.

6. The government has put price controls on bread.

7. Farmers are refusing to sell wheat for Dinars.

8. There are widespread shortages of bread produced by government-owned bakeries.

9. Seventy percent of Serbs are living below the poverty level.

10. Serbia may print a 5 million dinar note worth $1.00.

11. Because of the war, production is 30% of what it was the previous year.

12. Fifty percent of all industrial capacity is idle.

13. Only 1.4 million people are still at work. The remainder are in the military or are refugees.

14. Many workers are on the government payroll. They are not producing anything tangible.

15. In response to U.N. sanctions, the Serb government pledged that Serbs would not lose their jobs. So, many workers are on paid indefinite leave.

16. For every working person, there are two dependents on government aid.

17. Vital commodities such as flour, oil and sugar are rationed.

18. The economic sanctions prevent many spare parts from coming in. Gasoline is scarce.

19. Bread and other basics could soon disappear as state bakeries are out of flour. Private companies refuse to operate at a loss caused by price controls.

20. The next step may be factory kitchens because Serbs cannot provide workers with salaries that cover the cost of food.

21. In anticipation of winter food shortages, farmers are charging exorbitant prices for their fruit, vegetables and meat.

continued

List the item numbers in the appropriate column

Group #1	Group #2	Group #3
Aggregate demand	**Aggregate supply**	**Consequences of hyperinflation**
_____	_____	_____

As a team, agree on how you would illustrate what is happening in Serbia using an Aggregate demand/ Aggregate supply diagram.

Price Level

Real Output

Follow-up questions

1. Why are wars often associated with hyperinflation?

2. Why does hyperinflation lead to social chaos such as riots, and often leads to dictatorship?

3. Using last year as the base year, and an increase of 10 billion percent per year inflation, what would be the CPI in the current year?

4. (optional) Would you classify the hyperinflation in Serbia as demand-pull inflation, or cost-push inflation, or both?

5. (optional) Using the quantity theory of money as symbolized by the equation: $M \times V = P \times Q$, explain the cause of inflation in Serbia.

Economics
LIVE / 68

Counting GDP

Try Your Skill at Counting GDP!

(It takes thousands of employees at the
U.S. Department of Commerce to do the job.)

Included	Excluded
C - Consumer spending	U - Used (not produced this year)
I - Business investment including inventory	N - Non-market activities
G - Government purchases	T - Transfers (gift or exchange of paper assets)
E - Net exports	IN - Intermediate goods (goods used to produce other goods for final sale)

Card #	Category	Amount Excluded	Amount Included
1			
2			
3			
4			
5			
6			
7			
8			
9			
10			
11			
12			
13			
14			
15			
16			
17			
18			
		Total GDP	

Activity #39

Two sides of GDP

Teams

1. Number off in your group 1,2,3...

2. Below are the national income accounts for 1992. The problem is that they are all mixed up. Beginning with person number one, select one item and write it in the proper column below: is it an expenditure or an income item? Then person number two selects an item and places it in the proper column. Repeat until all items are listed. (All amounts in billions of dollars.)

Proprietors' income = $403   Consumption = $4096

Imports = $667   Rent = $61

Sales taxes = $552   Interest = $668

Investment = $771   Wages and salaries = $3223

Government = $1115   Depreciation = $651

Exports = $636   Corporate profits = $393

Expenditures	Incomes

3. When you have entered all the numbers, find out if you are correct. Add up the numbers in each column. If expenditures = incomes, explain why they must be equal. If not, brainstorm about which item or items was misplaced. Move it and then recalculate expenditures and incomes. Repeat until expenditures = incomes.

Teams

Reminder: Aggregate demand is the total demand for goods and services by consumers, businesses, government plus exports sales, all at a given price level.

Number off 1,2,3 and so on.

Assume the economy starts at point A.

Looking at Aggregate Demand

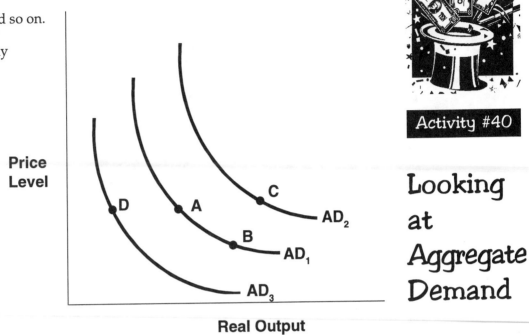

Real Output

Take turns reading each statement out loud. Then ask your teammates to match the statement to the letter on the graph. Start at point A.

Person 1: Fear of future layoffs causes consumer confidence to fall. Consumers cut their spending.

Pt. A to ____

Person 2: Prices are falling, so consumers' savings accounts have more purchasing power.

Pt. A to ____

Person 3: A recession is feared, so businesses cut inventory purchases.

Pt. A to ____

Person 4: The European economy is booming, so U.S. firms are selling lots of exports.

Pt. A to ____

Person 5: At a lower inflation rate, interest rates fall, so consumer and business spending increases.

Pt. A to ____

Person 6: To reduce the Federal deficit, income taxes are raised on consumers and businesses.

Pt. A to ____

Person 7: The stock market booms causing increased consumer wealth.

Pt. A to ____

Person 8: Consumer and business debt rises to extremely high levels.

Pt. A to ____

continued

Economics
LIVE / 71

Teams

Describe three specific events--not listed above--that would cause the aggregate demand curve to shift to the right and three events--not listed above--that would cause the aggregate demand curve to shift to the left.

Do not list them in order and do not indicate whether the aggregate demand curve shifts to the right or the left.

	Event	Shift right/left (leave blank)
1.		_____
2.		_____
3.		_____
4.		_____
5.		_____
6.		_____

Exchange this list with another group.

Other group: Fill in all the blank lines in the "shift right/shift left" column. Then pass the problem back to the original group to check if the answers are correct.

Teams

Reminder: Shifts in aggregate supply represent an increase or decrease in the economy's capacity to produce goods and services. For example, an increase in the economy's capacity to produce can be caused by:

- more labor or better skilled labor
- more capital goods (plant, equipment, machinery, construction, transportation and communications systems)
- better technology
- more natural resources
- lower costs of production for all firms because of lower natural resource prices, lower labor costs, lower costs of capital or increasing productivity.

Assume the economy starts at point A.

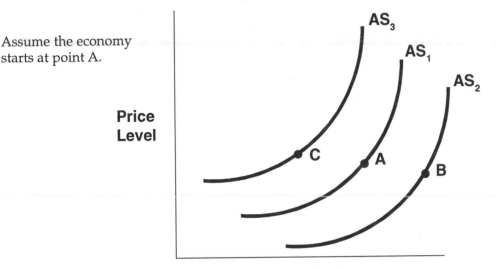

Shifting that Aggregate Supply Curve

Describe three specific events that would cause the aggregate supply curve to shift to point B and three specific events that would cause the aggregate supply curve to shift to point C. For example: "High reading scores plummet."

Do not list them in order and do not indicate whether the aggregate supply curve shifts to B or to C.

	Event	Shift to B or C (leave blank)
1.		
2.		
3.		
4.		
5.		
6.		

Exchange this list with another group.

Other group: Fill in the last column indicating a shift to B or C. Then return this sheet to the original group to check if the answers are correct.

© Keenan & Maier

Activity #42

Aggregate Supply Curve: 3 Views

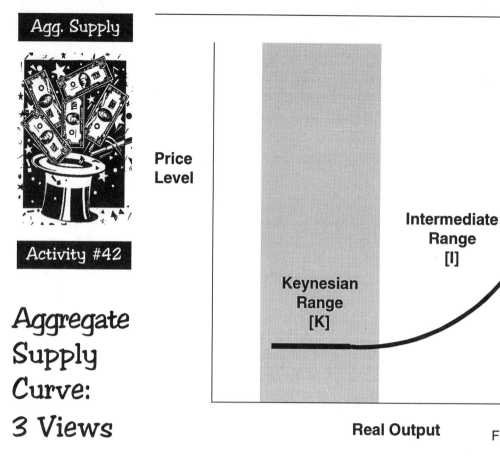

Reminder: Aggregate supply describes the relationship between total production and the price level.

Take turns reading a statement out loud. Ask your team members to match the statement with the correct range -- K, I or C -- on the aggregate supply curve.

Person 1: Because of a war, factories are operating at full capacity and are unable to produce any more goods. ☐

Person 2: A massive government spending program increases aggregate demand, but does not cause inflation. ☐

Person 3: Factories are operating with much unused capacity. ☐

Person 4: Pent-up consumer demand increases production and inflation. ☐

Person 5: There is high unemployment, including many experienced workers. ☐

Person 6: In a growing economy, firms find that their raw material costs rising and there are shortages of experienced labor. ☐

Person 7: A government spending program is causing the economy to produce more output, but with increasing prices as well. ☐

Teams

Using an aggregate demand-aggregate supply diagram, illustrate the following events in U.S. history. Label any shifts in the AD or AS lines by marking the starting price level and output level and final price level and output level.

Activity #43

For example:

1929-1933. During this time, the U.S. Federal Reserve Bank allowed the money supply to fall by 40%. This meant less money in circulation, fewer loans and higher interest rates. (Note: some economists believe this was the major cause of the Depression.)

U.S. Economic History with AD/AS

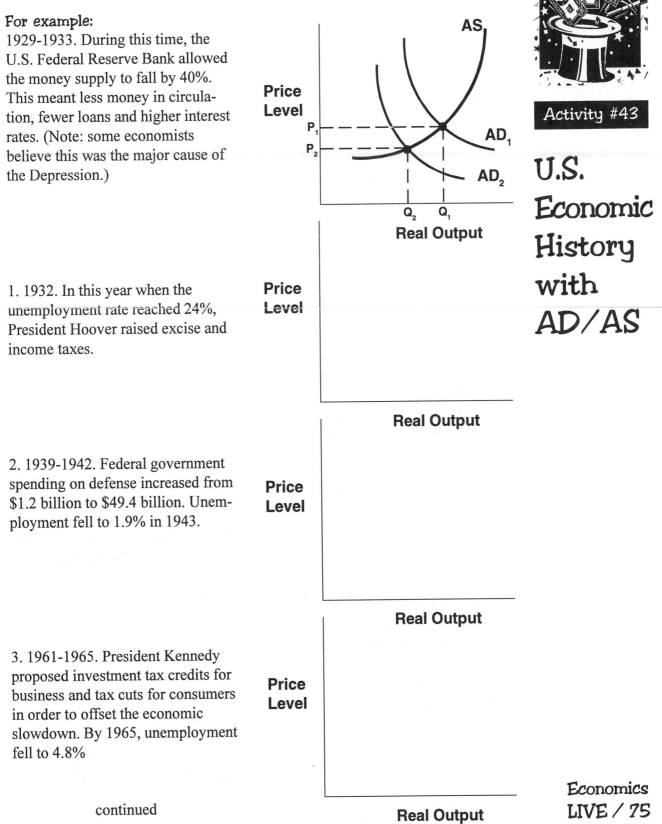

1. 1932. In this year when the unemployment rate reached 24%, President Hoover raised excise and income taxes.

2. 1939-1942. Federal government spending on defense increased from $1.2 billion to $49.4 billion. Unemployment fell to 1.9% in 1943.

3. 1961-1965. President Kennedy proposed investment tax credits for business and tax cuts for consumers in order to offset the economic slowdown. By 1965, unemployment fell to 4.8%

continued

4. 1965-1967. With the economy already at a high-employment level, the Federal government increased military spending for the Vietnam War from $49.4 billion to $71.5 billion. There was no offsetting tax hike. Inflation increased.

Price Level

Real Output

5. 1974-1978. With inflation already increasing, oil prices doubled in 1974, and then doubled again in 1978. The costs of production for all firms rose and consumers had less income for other purchases.

Price Level

Real Output

6. 1981-1984. The Reagan administration cut business and personal income taxes. Defense spending rose, but most non-defense spending fell.

Price Level

Real Output

7. 1991-1993. The Persian Gulf War caused a temporary increase in oil prices. Consumer confidence fell. Government spending increased only slightly during the war because most equipment came from existing inventories. European economies suffered severe recession and therefore purchased fewer U.S. goods.

Price Level

Real Output

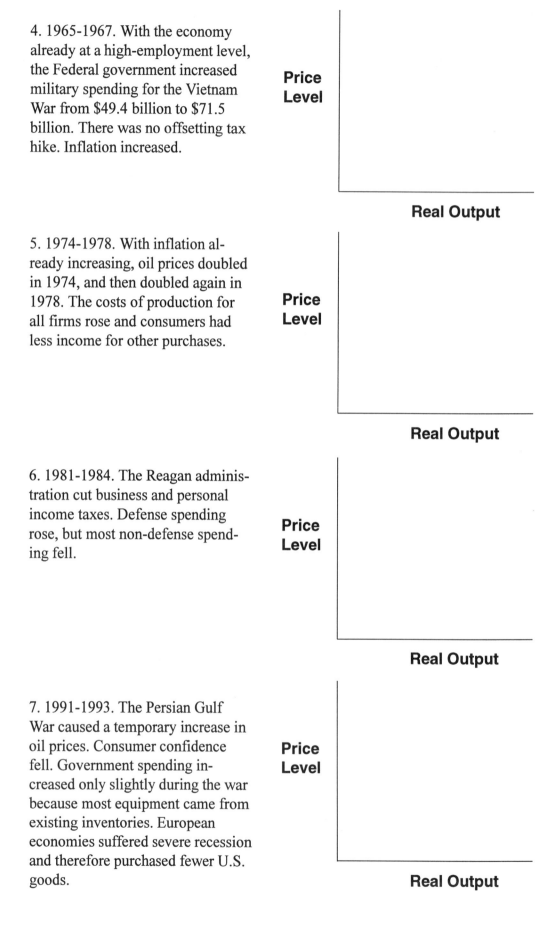

Most presidents propose an economic plan for the country. For example, President Clinton proposed a new U.S. economic program, designed to help the economy recover from recession and to increase U.S. global competitiveness.

1. **Stimulus package.** This includes investment tax credits for business, tax deductions for research and development, increased government spending on infrastructure (roads, bullet trains and telecommunications), increased spending on education, and extended unemployment benefits. The goal was to increase production and reduce unemployment.

2. **Long run deficit reduction.** This includes raising the income tax on the highest income group, increasing the Federal gasoline tax, an energy tax on all energy sources, cuts in government spending, especially defense and Medicare (health care for the elderly.) The goal was to reduce the size of the Federal government's deficit, running at more than $300 billion per year.

3. **The Clinton hope.** The stimulus package increases productivity because the government built needed infrastructure and private business investment created new research and development. The long run deficit reduction caused interest rates to fall so that there is even more business investment and productivity.

Clinton-omics

Teams

Divide your team into three groups.

Group 1:

Using an aggregate demand/aggregate supply diagram, illustrate the effects of the **stimulus plan**.

Price Level

Real Output

continued

© Keenan & Maier

Group 2:

Using an aggregate demand/aggregate supply diagram, illustrate the effects of the **deficit reduction plan**.

Price Level

Real Output

Group 3:

Using an aggregate demand/aggregate supply diagram, illustrate the effects of the **Clinton hope**.

Price Level

Real Output

All three groups: show your diagram to the other groups. Together agree on the *total*. You might want to consider short-run and long-run effects.

Follow-up question:

Is Clintonomics based on classical or Keynesian economy theory? Why?

Step 1

Individually survey yourself on the following:

    a) During the past year I have saved _____% of my total after tax income.
Therefore my aps = _____%; my apc = _____%.

    b) Imagine that you receive an unexpected check in the mail for $1,000, after taxes. During the year, how much of this $1,000 will you spend? $ _____; how much will you save? $ _____. Make certain that the sum is $1,000.

    Therefore my mpc = _____%;
my mps = _____%.

Teams

Step 2

Compare your results with others in your group.

	APC	APS	MPC	MPS
Student 1	___	___	___	___
Student 2	___	___	___	___
Student 3	___	___	___	___
Student 4	___	___	___	___
Average	___	___	___	___

Step 3

As a group answer the following questions:

1. For the U.S., the aps = 5%; apc = 95% Which is greater, your aps or the U.S. aps?

    Speculate why this might be true:

2. For the U.S., your textbook suggests an mps = 20%; the mpc = 80.% Which is greater, the your mps or the U.S. mps?

    Speculate why this might be true:

3. How would you answer the question about your mps and mpc, if you found an unexpected **bill** for $1,000 in your mailbox. Is your mpc the same or different for an unexpected reduction in your income compared with an unexpected increase in your income?

What's your MPC and APC

Is Keynes applicable today?

Teams

Your instructor will assign one or more of the following questions to your group. List evidence to support your position.

1. If your team had to identify the major lasting influence of Keynes, what would it be?

2. If your team had to identify the weakest part of the Keynesian economic theory, what would it be?

3. Do you think that Keynesian economic theory is the reason why the U.S. has not had another Great Depression?

4. Do you think that Keynesian economic theory is responsible for the current large Federal budget deficit?

5. During the 1970s, the economy was hit with high unemployment and high inflation. How well does Keynesian theory explain these events?

6. Give a Keynesian explanation of what might have caused the 1990-1991 recession.

Evidence for question number: ☐

1.

2.

3.

4.

5.

6.

At income level (Y)	Consumption (C)	Business Investment (I)	Total Spending
2000	1600	700	2300
2500	2000	700	2700
3000	2400	700	____
3500	2800	700	____
4000	____	700	3900
4500	3600	700	4300
5000	4000	700	4700
5500	____	700	5100
6000	4800	700	5500

Welcome to Macro-land

Teams

Welcome to Macroland. This is a simple economy with no government or foreign trade. Consumers and businesses in Macroland plan to produce according to the table below. As a team, answer the following:

1. What is the MPC?

2. What numbers go in the four blank spaces in the table above?

3. What is the equilibrium level of GDP? Why is this an equilibrium?

4. Why would $2500 not be an equilibrium?

> Total output is greater/less than demand?
> Inventories will rise/fall?
> Production plans will rise/fall?

5. Why would $5500 not be an equilibrium?

> Total output is greater/less than demand?
> Inventories will rise/fall?
> Production plans will rise/fall?

6. If full employment GDP is $4000, is this economy facing a recessionary or inflationary gap? Explain.

continued

7. What is the potential income multiplier in this economy?

8. If business investment increases to $900, what is the new equilibrium level of GDP?

9. Why did an increase of $200 in business investment cause a larger change in total spending in Macroland? (Answer *without* using the word "multiplier.")

10. If full employment is still $4000, with $900 business investment, is the economy facing a recessionary gap or an inflationary gap? Explain.

11. Divide your team into two groups:

   Group 1 -- Give a classical explanation for why this economy will recover.

   Group 2 - Give a Keynesian explanation for how this economy can recover.

Read your explanations to the other group.

12. (optional question) Graph Y, C, I and show the equilibrium level of income, first for I = $700, and then for I=$900.

13. (optional question) Solve for equilibrium GDP algebraically for I = $700 and I = $900. Assume that Yd=Y.

Teams

Step1
Your group will make up a problem for another group to solve. Fill in the blanks below based on the following:

• If most of your group are men, a = $100 billion ; if most of your group are women (or if you equal in numbers) a = $200 billion.

• If two people or more in your group wear glasses, I = $100 billion; if not, I = $200 billion.

• If everyone in your group has a brother or sister, G = $100 billion; if not G = $200.

• If everyone in your group is taller than 5′5" then mpc = 0.75; if not mpc = 0.8.

a (autonomous consumption) = _____   **I** (investment) = _____

G (government spending) = _____   **mpc** (marginal propensity to consume) = _____

Step 2
Pass this problem to another group as instructed.

Step 3
New group, fill in the chart using the numbers listed above.

The
Gap

If full employment income is $2000 billion is there (circle one):

• **recession**
• **inflation**
• **full employment**

If there is a recessionary or inflationary gap?

How large is the GDP gap?

(Output) Y	C	I	G	(Aggregate Spending) C + I + G	C +I + G = Y
0	___	___	___	___	___NO___
1000	___	___	___	___	___NO___
1200	___	___	___	___	___
1500	___	___	___	___	___
1600	___	___	___	___	___
2000	___	___	___	___	___
2400	___	___	___	___	___
2500	___	___	___	___	___
3000	___	___	___	___	___

Step 4
Pass the problem back to the group that designed it.

Step 5
Correct any errors in the answer.

Priming the pump

Teams

Step 1

Your group is the economic advisory council for the country of Macro. The current economic situation is as follows:

- Unemployment = 8%
- Inflation = 4%
- GDP = $7,000 billion
- Government deficit = $400 billion
- Real GDP growth rate for past year = -3%

Devise appropriate fiscal policies for the current year.

1. Type of fiscal policies: _____

2. Dollar amount of each policy: _____

3. Parts of government involved in making decisions about these policies:

4. What do you expect to occur because of your fiscal policies?

5. What could stall your plans? How long will it be from the time you make your decision until the policies affect the macroeconomy?

Step 2

Pass your decisions to another group as instructed.

New group: List as many reasons as you can why these fiscal policies may not work as planned.

Return this sheet to the original group for review.

Original group: Based on the problems listed above, how can you improve your fiscal policy?

Which problems will always exist with fiscal policy, no matter what you do?

Teams

As a group, work together to fill in the blank graph so that it corresponds to the diagram next to it. The AD/AS model goes on the left side and the Keynesian on the right.

Activity #50

Putting it all together

a) Inflationary gap

b) Increase in consumer confidence

c) Increase in autonomous consumption

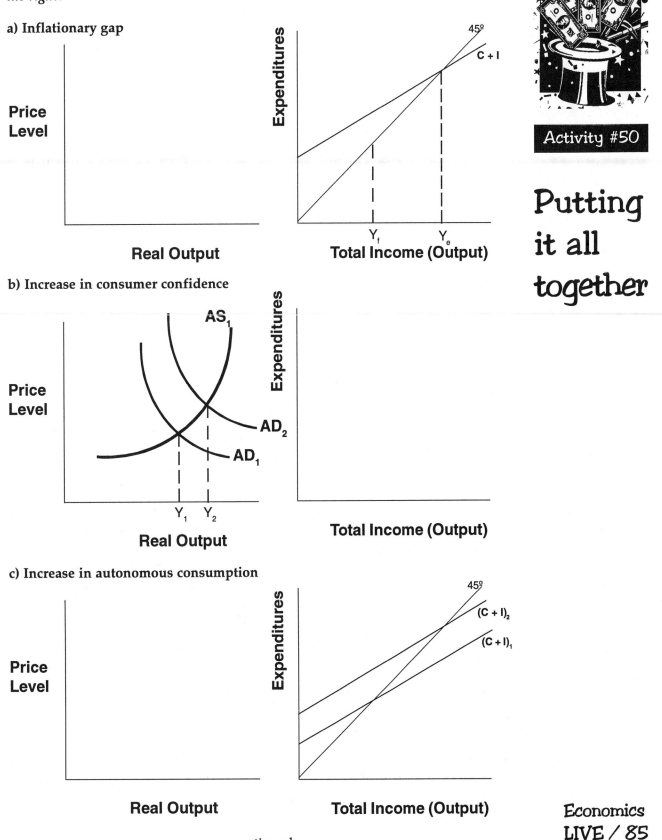

© Keenan & Maier   continued

d) Recessionary Gap

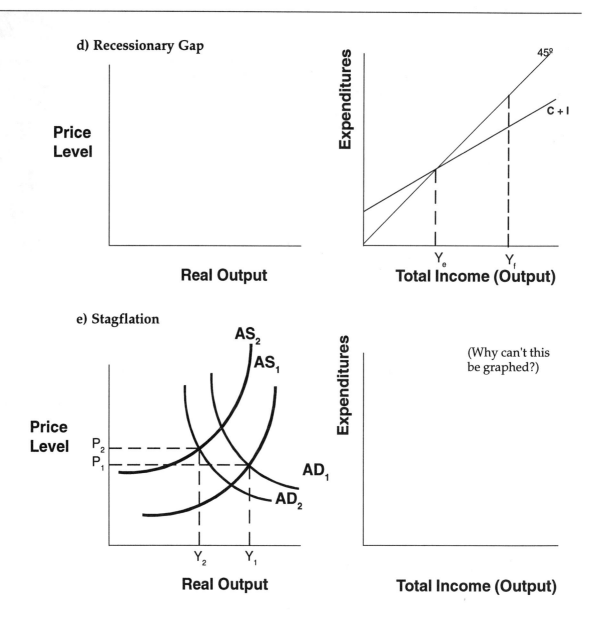

Price Level

Real Output

Expenditures

45°

C + I

Y_e Y_f

Total Income (Output)

e) Stagflation

AS_2

AS_1

Price Level

P_2
P_1

AD_1

AD_2

Y_2 Y_1

Real Output

Expenditures

(Why can't this be graphed?)

Total Income (Output)

f) Bonus question: Diagram an increase in the marginal propensity to consume.

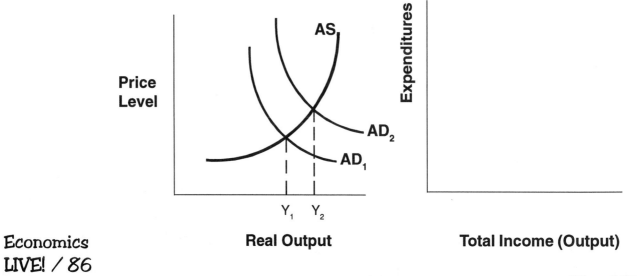

Price Level

AS_1

AD_2

AD_1

Y_1 Y_2

Real Output

Expenditures

Total Income (Output)

What effects do large Federal government deficits have on the economy? To better understand the possible consequences, consider a mythical land where the king is spending more than he collects in taxes. The story has four endings, each representing outcomes predicted by a different economic principle.

Count off in your group 1, 2, 3, 4. Everyone will read the story's beginning. Then read the ending corresponding to your number and decide which economic principle is represented here. Then check with your teammates to see if they agree.

Risky Deficits?

Beginning

Once a upon a time, in the Land Faraway, King Big Debt was spending big bucks on a new castle and moat. He needed more money fast. So he hot-footed it down to the town square, stood on his favorite soapbox, and announced he was selling Government Bonds, or G-Bills.

"Why should we buy the bonds from you?" the crowd yelled. King Big Debt pledged, "I'll pay good interest! 8%, 9%...okay I'll pay you 10% and the bonds are as secure as your currency."

People lined up to buy G-Bills. They were a better deal than the Faraway Bank or the Up and Down Stockmarket. King Big Debt continued to borrow & borrow until...

Endings

After reading the four possible endings on the following page, place the proper number in the corresponding box:

- [ ] **Keynesian**
- [ ] **Crowding out**
- [ ] **External debt**
- [ ] **Monetizing the debt**

continued

Ending # 1

One day the Private Crown Corporation decided to borrow to build a new factory. But the King had borrowed so much, there was little money left. The Private Crown Corporation and other businesses that wanted to expand found themselves bidding against one another for the small of amount of savings available for loans.

"I'll pay 10%," shouted one. "I'll pay 12%," shouted another. Interest rates skyrocketed. Private Crown Corporation cancelled its plan for a new factory. Others did the same. It wasn't long before the Faraway economy stagnated.

...THE END

Ending # 2

The King had a bright idea. He would print up some money! He was informed that most money was no longer currency but in bank checking deposits. So, he ordered the Royal Central Bank to buy all the G-Bills and credit his account so that he could pay his bills.

With all the money earned in government projects, the town went on a buying spree. Shops were bustling and shopkeepers couldn't keep up with orders. It wasn't long before prices in Faraway went up, up, up. Coach prices soared and castles were soon out of reach of young Farawayians. Inflation had come to Faraway.

...THE END

Ending # 3

Prior to the King's building program, the economy had languished in recession. Unemployment had been above 7% and businesses were discouraged from investing in new plant and equipment because of the poor business outlook.

After the King's program, employment picked up not only in castle and moat building, but also across the economy because businesses were more optimistic about the future and started to expand their capacity. The Faraway economy boomed.

...THE END

Ending #4

Banks and wealthy individuals in Nearby, a land north of Faraway, heard of high interest rates and wanted to invest in G-Bills too. So, they hot-footed it down to their investment brokers and bought a high percentage of the G-bills. As a result, there were savings in Faraway available for lending to Faraway corporations, so interest rates fell back to 8%.

Years later, Nearby investors started to sell the G-bills and used the proceeds to buy things in Faraway. Soon, Faraway citizens found that their most desirable goods and services were being exported to Nearby, and that Faraway real estate and businesses were owned by foreigners.

...THE END

Follow-up team questions

1. Assume all the endings are possible, which do you think would have the most negative effects on the economy? Why?

2. The U.S. government currently is running large deficits. Do you observe any of the consequences described in these endings?

3. Is there another ending to this story that you think should be added? Describe it.

The Growing Debt

*The table below summarizes the growth of the U.S. Federal debt since 1791 in **millions of dollars.***

Teams

As a group, answer the following questions:

1. Find two time periods when the debt decreased.

2. Find four time periods when the debt increased rapidly.

3. Provide a historical explanation for each of these changes:

Debt decreased:

1. (years_____) 2. (years_____)

Debt increased:

1. (years_____) 3. (years_____)

2. (years_____) 4. (years_____)

National Debt	
1835	0
1850	63
1865	2,678
1890	1,122
1900	1,263
1915	1,191
1920	24,299
1930	16,185
1940	42,967
1945	258,682
1960	286,331
1970	370,919
1980	914,300
1985	1,827,500
1990	3,163,000
1995	5,176,000

4. The data presented here exaggerates the growth of the debt. Why? (Hint: what else increased since 1835?)

5. How could you correct this table so it more accurately measures the effect of the debt on the economy?

Step 1

Individually complete the survey at the bottom of the page. *Do not put your name on the survey.* Your instructor will collect the survey.

Step 2

Individually, give a one sentence definition of:

M1:

M2:

What's Your M2

Step 3

Given the data for the class, calculate the class--

M1:

M2:

M1 / M2 ratio:

- -

Student Survey (no names!)

Please estimate how much you currently have in the following forms of money:

currency: _____   **checking accounts (all types):** _____

savings accounts (all types): _____

continued

Economics
LIVE / 91

© Keenan & Maier

Step 4

M1 for the U.S. is now about (consult your textbook):

M2 for the U.S. is now about (consult your textbook):

The ratio of M1/M2 for the U.S. is:

Compare your answers with the rest of your group.

Compare the ratio of M1/M2 for the class and for the U.S. Which is higher?

Brainstorm in your group for reasons why the ratio for the class differs from the ratio for the U.S. This is true because:

Teams

Designate two "starters." The "starter" is person number 1 for each problem. Pass problem # 1 below to the right. Pass problem # 2 to the left. Then come together at the end to answer the follow-up questions.

Problem # 1: (reserve requirement = 20%)

You take $500 from your piggy bank and deposit it at University Bank.

University Bank			
Assets	**Liabilities**	**Δ in Deposits**	**Δ in M1**
Required reserves $100	$500	+$500	$0
Excess reserves $400			

Person 1 -- University bank loans $400 to Cash Starved Sam. Sam deposits it in Bank of America.

Bank of America			
Assets	**Liabilities**	**Δ in Deposits**	**Δ in M1**

Creating money

Person 2 -- Bank of America loans its excess reserves to Disneyland Corporation. Disney deposits in Wells Fargo Bank.

Wells Fargo Bank			
Assets	**Liabilities**	**Δ in Deposits**	**Δ in M1**

Person 3 -- Wells Fargo loans its excess reserves to Madonna. She deposits it in Chase Manhattan Bank.

Chase Manhattan			
Assets	**Liabilities**	**Δ in Deposits**	**Δ in M1**

Person 4 -- Chase loans its excess reserves to IBM. IBM deposits it in Citibank.

Citibank			
Assets	**Liabilities**	**Δ in Deposits**	**Δ in M1**

Stop. How much in loans has been made based on the initial deposit of $500?

© Keenan & Maier

J.P. Morgan

Assets		Liabilities	Δ in Deposits	Δ in M1
Required reserves	$200	$2000	+$2000	$0
Excess reserves	$1800			

Banco Bank

Assets	Liabilities	Δ in Deposits	Δ in M1

New York Bank

Assets	Liabilities	Δ in Deposits	Δ in M1

Magic Kingdom Bank

Assets	Liabilities	Δ in Deposits	Δ in M1

1st Interstate Bank

Assets	Liabilities	Δ in Deposits	Δ in M1

Problem # 2

Your aunt in Mexico sent you a check for $2,000. You deposit in your bank at J.P. Morgan. Reserve requirements are 10%

Person 1 -- J.P. Morgan loans its excess reserves to Donald Trump. He deposits it in Banco Bank.

Person 2 -- Banco Bank loans its excess reserves to Woody Allen. Woody deposits it in New York Bank.

Person 3 -- New York Bank loans its excess reserves to Donald Duck. Donald deposits the money at Magic Kingdom Bank.

Person 4 -- Magic Kingdom Bank loans its excess reserves to Goofy. Goofy deposits the check at First Interstate Bank.

Stop. How much in loans has been made based on the initial deposit of $2,000?

Follow-up questions

1. Based on problem # 1, with the reserve requirement of 20%:

   How much in new loans are created if the process continues forever?   (Hint: Total new loans = initial excess reserves x money multiplier)

2. Based on problem # 2, with the reserve requirement of 10%:

   What is the total of new loans if the process continues forever?

3. If the Federal Reserve Bank wanted to increase the money supply it could _____ the reserve requirement.

Who runs the FED?

Step 1

Individually, draw a diagram that illustrates the relationship between the following parts of the Federal Reserve:

- **Chair of the Board of Governors**
- **Seven Board of Governors**
- **Twelve member Federal Open Market Committee**

Step 2

Compare your diagram with others in the group. Combine the best features of each diagram to improve your diagram above.

continued

Step 3

As a group, add to your diagram an explanation of how each part of the Federal Reserve is chosen. Use the following terms in your explanations:

- U.S. President
- U.S. Senate
- Member banks of the Federal Reserve
- New York Federal Reserve President
- District Federal Reserve Bank President

Step 4

As a group, add to your diagram the location where the following monetary policy decisions are made:

- Discount rate
- Reserve requirements
- Buying and selling government bonds in the open market

Question:

What are the advantages and disadvantages of the way in which the U.S. Federal Reserve is organized?

Advantages	Disadvantages

Changing the reserve ratio

Teams

Step 1

You will make up a problem for another person. Fill in the blanks below for a mythical country. You may use any reasonable numbers. Assume that no bank has excess reserves.

At the start total bank deposits = $___ billion

The old required reserve ratio = __%

The new required reserve ratio = __%

Pass this problem to another person as directed by your instructor.

Step 2

Answering person: Fill in the blanks based on the information above.

1. Required reserves with the **old** required reserve ratio = $_____

2. Total reserves with old required reserve ratio = required reserves + excess reserves = $_____ (Remember: excess reserves = $0 to start.)

3. Required reserves with the **new** required reserve ratio = $_____

4. Excess reserves = total reserves (at start) - required reserves (with new required reserve ratio) = $_____ (May be a negative number.)

5. Will banks increase or decrease lending?

6. The money multiplier with the new required reserve ratio =_____

7. The amount of added or subtracted lending capacity = excess reserves x money multiplier = $_____

8. Total potential bank deposits = original bank deposits + new lending capacity = $_____

Step 3

Return the problem to the first person to check for errors.

Monetary policy-- step by step

Open market operations

Teams

Step 1

Pick a partner. Person A fills in the left-side blanks. Person B fills in the right-side blanks.

Person A	Person B
FED buys bonds	**FED sells bonds**

Initially: **Initially:**

Bank deposits = $ 1000 billion   Bank deposits = $1000 billion

Required reserve ratio = 10%   Required reserve ratio = 10%

Initial required reserves =_____   Initial required reserves =_____

Excess reserves = $ 0   Excess reserves = $0

Then: **Then:**

FED buys $10 billion in bonds   FED sells $10 billion in
    from the public   bonds to the public

Bank deposits = $_____   Bank deposits = $990 billion

Total bank reserves = $110 billion   Total bank reserves = $90 billion

Required reserves = $101 billion   Required reserves =_____

Excess reserves =_____   Excess reserves = - $9 billion

Money multiplier =_____   Money multiplier =_____

Change in lending   Change in lending
    capacity = $90 billion   capacity =_____

New level of bank   New level of bank
    deposits =_____   deposits = $900 billion

Step 2

Exchange answers and check to see if they are correct.

Step 1

Your group is the economic advisory council for the country of Macro. The current economic situation is as follows:

- Unemployment = 5%
- Prime interest rate = 16%
- Discount rate = 12%
- Real GDP growth rate for past year = +3%

- Inflation = 10%
- Growth of M1 = 14%

Manag- ing Mone- tary Policy

Devise appropriate monetary policies for the current year.

1. Type of monetary policy or policies:

2. Who decides these policies in the U.S.?

3. What do you expect to occur because of your monetary policies?

4. What could stall your plans? How long will it be from the time you make your decisions until the policies affect the macroeconomy?

continued

Step 2

Pass your decisions to the group on your left.

New group: List all the problems you see that may occur because of the monetary policies chosen above.

Return this sheet to the original group for review.

Original Group: Based on the problems listed above, how can you improve your monetary policy?

Which problems will always exist with monetary policy, no matter what you do?

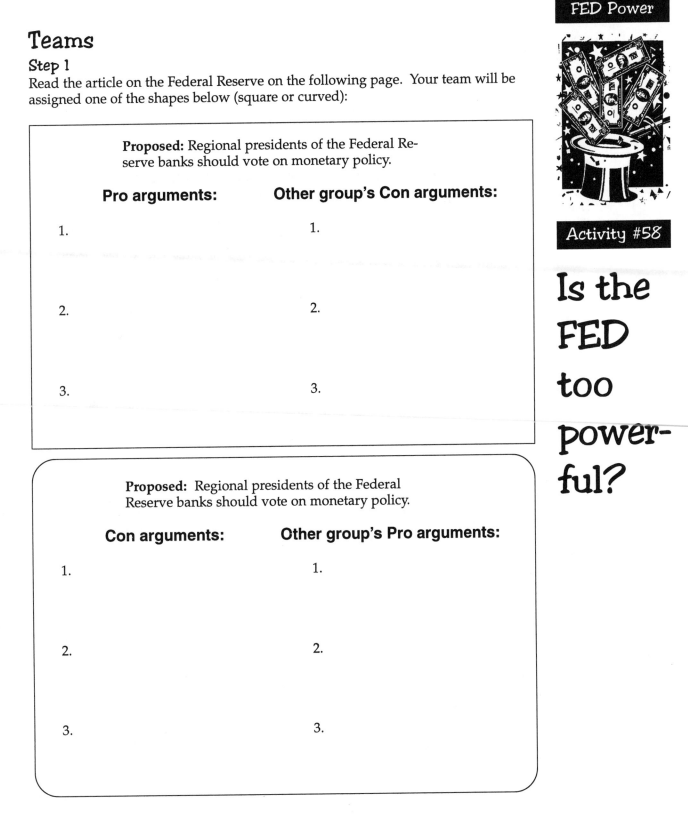

Teams

Step 1
Read the article on the Federal Reserve on the following page. Your team will be assigned one of the shapes below (square or curved):

Proposed: Regional presidents of the Federal Reserve banks should vote on monetary policy.

Pro arguments:	**Other group's Con arguments:**
1.	1.
2.	2.
3.	3.

Proposed: Regional presidents of the Federal Reserve banks should vote on monetary policy.

Con arguments:	**Other group's Pro arguments:**
1.	1.
2.	2.
3.	3.

Step 2
"Pro" pair find a "Con" pair to make a group of four. Pro side reads 3 arguments to con side. Con side records. Then con side reads 3 arguments to pro side. Pro side records.

Step 3
Choose by consensus the best argument on each side.

continued

Is the FED too powerful?

"Critics Want Fed's Power Under More Accountability"

by David Rosenbaum, *New York Times*, November 14, 1991

The Federal Reserve holds an anomalous position in the American system. An enormously powerful Government agency, it is only loosely accountable to the public and to elected officials, and it allows private citizens, basically a banking elite, to help set the Government's economic policy.

When the economy is sour, as it is now, this odd structure tends to become a focus of attention, a sponge that soaks up frustrations over the way the economy is going.

Critics of the central bank had a new twist this morning. At a Senate hearing, several prominent lawmakers, an economist who holds a Nobel Prize and a former vice chairman of the Federal Reserve Board testified in favor of legislation to make the agency more politically accountable. The measure would prevent the presidents of the regional Federal Reserve banks, who hold no Government office and answer to no Government official, from voting on Government policy as they do now.

The bill is not likely to be enacted, at least not any time soon, but the legislation has stirred up a new debate on the extent to which the Fed operates outside the bounds of an open society.

"Power without accountability does not fit the American system of democracy," said Representative Lee H. Hamilton, an Indiana Democrat who is a frequent critic of the Federal Reserve and one of the widely respected members of Congress.

Teams

You are responsible for managing a hypothetical economy. **Your goal is to achieve a steady increase in real GDP of 3% per year.**

Step 1

Separate the policy cards from the number cards. Shuffle the number cards and place them face down.

Step 2

Pick one policy card. Decide together if the policy card is an example of a monetary or fiscal policy. Decide together whether you want to increse or decrease this policy and whether it will change GDP up or down. Record these results in the table below.

Step 3

Pick one number card from the face-down pile. This card measures the effect of your policy. **For example:**

	Card	Fiscal or Monetary	Increase or Decrease	Δ in GDP (+ or -)	Dollar Change
1.	Tax	Fiscal	Increase	-	$20 billion

Step 4

On the economy chart (next page) place a mark in column one above or below "0" based on your dollar change in GDP. This will be your starting point for the game.

Step 5

Choose another policy card so that you can move your economy toward the 3% growth path. Choose another number card to find out the effect of this policy. Record these results in the table below and on economy chart in column 2.

Step 6

Repeat step 5 until you have used all the policy cards. Use each policy card only once and keep the number cards face down.

Control-ling the Economy

	Card	Fiscal or Monetary	Increase or Decrease	Δ in GDP (+ or -)	Dollar Change
1					
2					
3					
4					
5					
6					
7					
8					
9					
10					

Names in Group:

Warning: There will be one 'external shock' to your economy announced by your instructor during the game.

continued

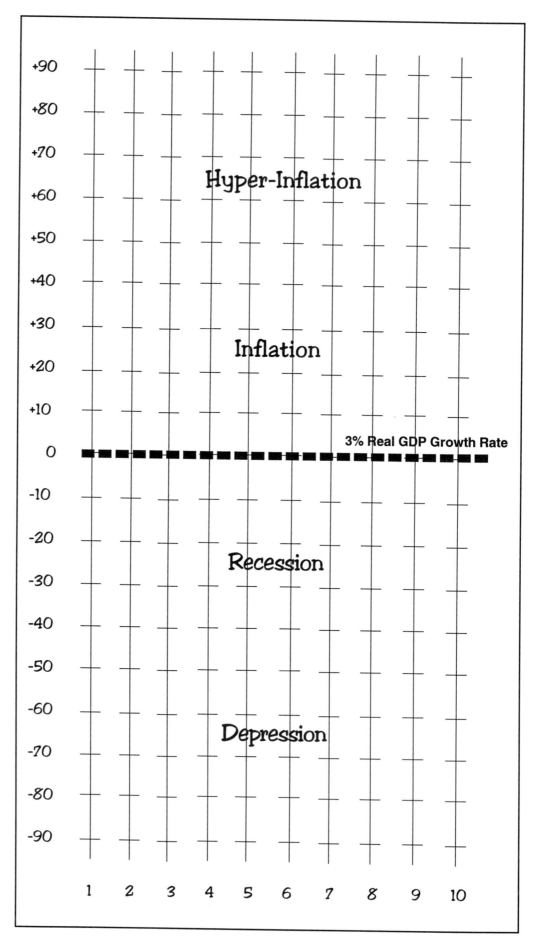

Follow-up Questions

1. Were you able to achieve a steady growth of 3% in real GDP? If not, what problems did you experience?

2. Why is the 3% growth rate a desirable goal? Why would a 'stable' 0% growth rate be undesirable?

3. Illustrate three rounds of your game using aggregate demand and aggregate supply curves.

Round _____

Round _____

Round _____

continued

4. In the game, the economy can be in depression, recession, inflation or hyperinflation. What economic problem is impossible in the design of the game?

5. In the game, policies have unknown effects. Give some examples of unknown effects in the real world?

Teams

Form teams of two. For this exercise you need a watch or clock, any book and some pieces of scrap paper.

Step 1
Time your partner for 30 seconds, counting how many pages he or she can turn one at a time using one hand.

	Person 1	Person 2
# of page turns		
# of paper folds		

Step 2
Time your partner to see how many folds he or she can make in a piece of paper in 30 seconds using one hand. (Unfolding the paper after each fold.)

Step 3
Compare your results with your partner.

Who has an **absolute** advantage in page turning? _____

In paper folding? _____

Who has a **comparative** advantage in page turning? _____
Explain:

Who has a **comparative** advantage in paper folding? _____
Explain:

Step 4
1. In the theory of international trade, absolute advantage means?

- In the theory of international trade, comparative advantage means?

2. Describe a situation in which the principle of comparative advantage is used to determine which person will do which task. Your example may come from a workplace, a sport or your household.

Comparative advantage in paperfolding?

The fluctuat-ing dollar

Teams

Step 1

Number your team 1, 2, 3 and so on.

Step 2

Each team member will write a short explanation for **why** the following occurred:

Person # 1 -- U.S. exports fall
Person # 2 -- U.S. interest rates rise
Person # 3 -- U.S. investment abroad increases
Person # 4 -- U.S. imports fall
Person # 5 -- U.S. inflation rate falls
Person # 6 -- Foreign investment in the U.S. decreases

For example: If you were assigned "exports rise," you might write:

"U.S. musical styles become a worldwide favorite."

Use your imagination! **Do not use the value of the dollar in your explanation.**

Your story:

Step 3

Together, match the stories of each teammate with one of the graphs below.

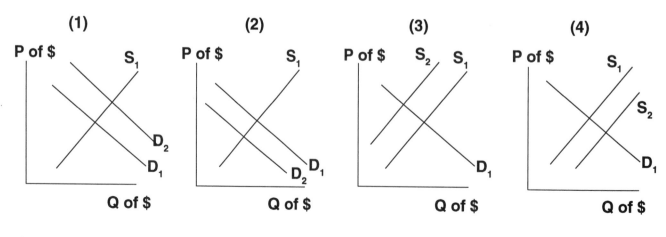

Teams

Step 1
After reading the article on the following page your team will be assigned one of the shapes below (square or curved):

Proposed: The U.S. should impose tariffs on imported footwear.

Pro arguments:	Other group's Con arguments:
1.	1.
2.	2.
3.	3.

Proposed: The U.S. should impose tariffs on imported footwear.

Con arguments:	Other group's Pro arguments:
1.	1.
2.	2.
3.	3.

Free trade?

Step 2
"Pro" pair find a "Con" pair to make a group of four. Pro side reads 3 arguments to con side. Con side records. Then con side reads 3 arguments to pro side. Pro side records.

Step 3
Choose by consensus the best argument on each side.

© Keenan & Maier

continued

"The New Free-Trade Heel"
by Jeffrey Ballinger, *Harper's Magazine*, August, 1992

In the 1980s, Oregon-based Nike closed its last U.S. footwear factory in Saco, Maine, while establishing most of its new factories in South Korea. Nike's actions were part of the broader "globalization" trend that saw the United States lose 65,300 footwear jobs between 1982 and 1989 as shoe companies sought non-unionized Third World workers who didn't require the U.S. rubber-shoe industry average of $6.94 an hour. But in the late 1980s, South Korean laborers gained the right to form independent unions and to strike. Higher wages ate into Nike's profits. The company shifted new factories to poorer countries such as Indonesia, where labor rights are generally ignored and wages are but one-seventh of South Korea's.

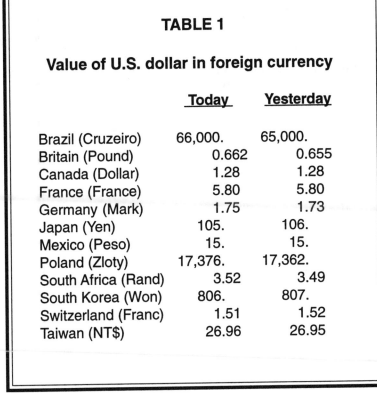

TABLE 1

Value of U.S. dollar in foreign currency

	Today	Yesterday
Brazil (Cruzeiro)	66,000.	65,000.
Britain (Pound)	0.662	0.655
Canada (Dollar)	1.28	1.28
France (France)	5.80	5.80
Germany (Mark)	1.75	1.73
Japan (Yen)	105.	106.
Mexico (Peso)	15.	15.
Poland (Zloty)	17,376.	17,362.
South Africa (Rand)	3.52	3.49
South Korea (Won)	806.	807.
Switzerland (Franc)	1.51	1.52
Taiwan (NT$)	26.96	26.95

Teams

Step 1

Individually: Find a currency that appreciated relative to the dollar in Table 1 at the top of the page.

Step 2

Individually: Find a currency that depreciated relative to the dollar

Step 3

As a group, compare your answers to 1 and 2. For which country did the currency appreciate the most?

For which country did the currency depreciate the most?

continued

Economics
LIVE / 111

© Keenan & Maier

TABLE 2

Country	A Weight of trade with U.S.	B % change in value of US$	C Column A x Column B
Canada	.30	0%	_____
Japan	.30	-1%	_____
Mexico	.15	0%	_____
Germany	.10	+1%	_____
Britain	.10	+1%	_____
France	.05	0%	_____
(Trade Weighted Index) **Sum =**			_____

Step 4
Trade weighted index

The Table 2 above lists the top six countries trading with the U.S. The "weight of trade" is the proportion of trade with each country, including both imports and exports.

Notice the trade weighted index adds the change in each currency's value multiplied by the share of trade with that country.

Calculate the trade weighted index. First multiply percent changes in currency values by the relative amount of trade each country does with the U.S. (These weights are provided in column B.) Then, add up all the numbers in the last column.

Overall has the dollar appreciated or depreciated?

Follow-up question:

Based on the trade weighted index in this example, what do you predict will happen to the sale of U.S. imports and exports?